The Promise of
Endless Summer

The Promise of Endless Summer

Cricket Lives from
The Daily Telegraph

Edited by Martin Smith

Aurum

First published 2013 by
Aurum Press Limited
74-77 White Lion Street
Islington
London N1 9PF
www.aurumpress.co.uk

Copyright © 2013 Telegraph Media Group Limited
Introduction Copyright © 2013 Martin Smith

The moral right of Martin Smith to be identified as the Editor of this work has been asserted by him in accordance with the Copyright, Designs and Patents Act 1988.

All rights reserved. No part of this book may be reproduced or utilised in any form or by any means, electronic or mechanical, including photocopying, recording or by any information storage and retrieval system, without permission in writing from Aurum Press Ltd.

Every effort has been made to contact the copyright holders of material in this book. However, where an omission has occurred, the publisher will gladly include acknowledgement in any future edition.

A catalogue record for this book is available from the British Library.

ISBN 978 1 78131 048 9

10 9 8 7 6 5 4 3 2 1
2017 2016 2015 2014 2013

Typeset by SX Composing DTP, Rayleigh, Essex SS6 7XF

Printed and bound in Great Britain by MPG Printgroup, UK

*For my progeny, Alexander, William and Poppy,
all hard-working students at universities around the country*

Contents

Introduction	ix
Don Bradman	1
W.F. Deedes	
Bill Ponsford	4
E.W. Swanton	
Sydney Copley	6
E.W Swanton	
Bill O'Reilly	7
E.W. Swanton	
R.E.S. Wyatt	10
Harold Larwood	13
Michael Parkinson	
Bill Voce	19
E.W. Swanton	
Bill Bowes	21
E.W. Swanton	
Norman Mitchell-Innes	23
Syed Mushtaq Ali	25
H.D. Read	27
Ron Hamence	29
Ernie Toshack	31
Ray Lindwall	34
Len Hutton	36
Cyril Washbrook	38
Keith Miller	41
Michael Parkinson	
Denis Compton	44
John Major	
Denis Compton	46
Michael Parkinson	
Bill Edrich	48
E.W. Swanton	
Sam Loxton	50
Kenneth Cranston	53
Lindsay Hassett	55
E.W. Swanton	
Les Ames	58
E.W. Swanton	
Godfrey Evans	60
Michael Henderson	
Keith Andrew	64
Arthur McIntyre	67
Gil Langley	70
John Waite	72

Trevor Bailey	74	**Fred Trueman**	128
Alec Bedser	78	Scyld Berry	
Derek Pringle		**Brian Statham**	132
Peter Loader	82	Michael Henderson	
Eric Bedser	84	**Derek Shackleton**	135
Stuart Surridge	87	David Green	
E.W. Swanton		**Butch White**	137
Tony Lock	89	**Colin Ingleby-Mackenzie**	141
Christopher Martin-Jenkins		**Bryan 'Bomber' Wells**	144
Peter May	91	**Bill Alley**	148
E.W. Swanton		**Ken Suttle**	151
Charles Palmer	93	**The Nawab of Pataudi**	154
Bert Sutcliffe	96	**Jack Flavell**	157
Clyde Walcott	98	**Geoff Griffin**	160
Scyld Berry		**Basil D'Oliveira**	163
Alf Valentine	100	Scyld Berry	
Colin Croft		**John Arlott**	169
Subhash Gupte	103	Tony Lewis	
Dennis Brookes	105	**Brian Johnston**	172
Frank Parr	108	**Bill Frindall**	174
T.C. 'Dickie' Dodds	111	**Colin Milburn**	177
Colin Cowdrey	115	Tony Lewis	
Michael Henderson		**Arthur Milton**	179
Colin Cowdrey	117	David Green	
David Sheppard		**Fred Titmus**	181
The Right Reverend Lord Sheppard of Liverpool	121	Scyld Berry	
Les Jackson	125	**Don Wilson**	184

Roy McLean	187	**Sylvester Clarke**	212
		Simon Hughes	
Russell Endean	189		
		Graham Dilley	215
Eddie Barlow	192	Derek Pringle	
Tony Greig	194	**David Bairstow**	218
		Michael Parkinson	
Roy Fredericks	198		
		Peter Roebuck	220
Bob Woolmer	200	Derek Pringle	
Scyld Berry			
		Hansie Cronje	223
Tom Cartwright	203	**E.W. Swanton**	226
David Green		Scyld Berry	
David Shepherd	206	**Christopher Martin-Jenkins**	230
Derek Pringle		Derek Pringle	
Malcolm Marshall	209	**George Pope**	233
Mark Nicholas		Michael Parkinson	

Introduction

It is not often that the death of a cricketer puts a temporary brake on affairs of state. However, the departure of the player who perhaps epitomised best the Britain of 'long shadows on county grounds [and] warm beer', brought a brief interlude in frenetic canvassing during the 1997 General Election campaign for the Leader of the Conservative Party. Just eight days before polling was due to begin, the Right Honourable John Major, M.P., took time out to compose for the *Daily Telegraph* a tribute to his boyhood hero Denis Compton, whose death had just been announced. To put it in its historical context, the incumbent prime minister was fighting for his future amid a frenzied atmosphere of political infighting, particularly over Europe, sleaze allegations against party members and an increasingly centralist Labour Party intent on taking advantage. Yet Major sheltered, metaphorically at least, beneath the hustings to write a heartfelt piece which appeared on the leader page of the following day's newspaper. In it he turned back the clock fifty years, just as he had done in his 1993 speech about Britishness and warm beer, only this time to evoke fond memories of a golden age for cricket. 'Denis personified the romance of cricket,' Major wrote. 'He was a hero to most males now over the age of forty-five, and his dashing batting and good looks had an appeal to the ladies, too,' he continued. 'Throughout my boyhood he put to the sword

– often nearly single-handedly – the best talent from South Africa, Australia and the West Indies.' He concluded: 'He was an Olympian of cricket. Thank you, Denis. You left memories for all time, even for those who only saw you from afar.'

In a few hundred well-chosen words, Major captured the appeal not only of D.C.S. Compton but also the appeal of cricket itself. It is a sport bound up in nostalgia and wistfulness for the black-and-white days when our heroes took off their demob suits and donned pristine flannels to face the best the Empire could throw at us. Cricket in the immediate post-War years continues to be viewed through a golden filter, helped no doubt by the long, hot summer of 1947 and the arrival of Don Bradman's impossibly glamorous, and apparently invincible, Australians the following year. The public were weary after six years of war and the cricketers put on a show that not only quickened the pulse but also underlined a *joie de vivre* that was palpable. Many of the players had seen active service during the Second World War and it may be no coincidence that the game's most colourful characters – Compton, Edrich and Miller – were among them. The overwhelming feeling was one of relief just to have survived the conflict, and they put their backs and shoulders into expressing that relief. Compton had served with the Army in India; Bill Edrich rose to become a Squadron Leader in Bomber Command, and was rewarded with the Distinguished Flying Cross; Keith Miller flew Mosquitos over Germany with Messerschmitts hanging on to his tail (though he put it rather more robustly than that!) In 1947, Compton and Edrich compiled 7,355 runs between them for Middlesex and England, Compton including eighteen centuries in his 3,816 aggregate. Miller, the golden boy of Australia, greatly enriched the Victory Test series in 1945 and the Ashes series of 1948. No wonder the short-trousered, future prime minister was smitten.

Stories of the feats and deeds of those demob-happy cricketers have been handed down over the years, some doubtlessly embellished but none the worse for that. It is the essence of cricket; it is what makes bearable the endless winter nights when deckchairs, picnic hampers and binoculars have long since been stowed away. In his appreciation of M.C. Cowdrey, the opening paragraph of which not only forms the preface to this book, but also provides its title, Michael Henderson talks about 'a memory, intangible yet always present, of the game as it was and as it can be, like some promise of endless summer'. As cricket-lovers we have a tendency to look back through rose-tinted glasses to days when the sun always shone, the game was played by gentlemen and England were always 302 for two at tea. We conveniently forget the frequent 'rain stopped play' signs, the bouncers and beamers of certain Test series and the fact that Australia once ran up 404 for the loss of three wickets in the fourth innings to win an Ashes match at Headingley. Miller contributed just a dozen runs to that innings, incidentally. Cricket can take you off in tangential directions at times. Here's proof: Miller's wicket in that fourth Test in 1948 was taken by Kenneth Cranston, an amateur who 'set aside' two post-War summers to play cricket. And to a reasonable standard, too: he captained both Lancashire and England before 'retiring', as planned, to the family dental business. He died in 2007 and his sporting curriculum vitae is included within these pages.

At this point it is probably worth establishing the parameters for what is ostensibly a celebration of cricketers past, particularly if you were hoping to read a eulogy to, say, W.G. Grace, C.B. Fry or J.B. Hobbs. They died in 1915, 1956 and 1963 respectively, and were naturally accorded fulsome, if slightly staid, death notices in the *Telegraph*. But until the mid-1980s, when Max Hastings became the paper's editor, there had been no separate obituaries section as we know it today and reports of deaths took their chances amid the news selection of the day; consequently, they were generally much shorter, terser and gave little idea of the personality beyond the bare bones of their careers. Hastings appointed Hugh Massingberd to produce a daily obituaries page, and under him obituary writing was revolutionised. Though customarily unsigned, they became, as they still are, pieces of writing to rival any in the paper, full of colourful anecdote, mordant wit and trenchant judgments and, quite simply, an essential feature of the *Telegraph*.

Cricket could have been made for Massingberd's new rubric, and indeed cricketers became a staple of his new order. While catching the big fish of the sport from the 1930s through to the 1960s, plus a few who played during the 1970s and later, the selection for this book has been mainly compiled from the Massingberd era. Some much longer pieces have been condensed for reasons of space, with the intention of bringing out the illuminating stories and insights that explain why the subject originally caught the imagination. These obituaries are complemented by a great many more pieces – tributes, memoirs and elegies – mostly published on the sports pages of the *Daily* and the *Sunday Telegraph*, from those who knew the subject well and in many cases played with or against him.

The articles are compiled not in chronological order by date of death, or even alphabetically, but in a way that juxtaposes and dovetails with contemporary team-mates, opponents, matches and events. The book begins with W.F. Deedes's musings on his first sighting of Don Bradman in 1930, quickly followed by The Don's pre-War colleagues like Bill Ponsford and Bill O'Reilly, as well as opponents R.E.S. Wyatt, Harold Larwood and Bill Voce, before moving on to post-War contemporaries such as Ray Lindwall, Ron Hamence, Ernie Toshack, Len Hutton, Sam Loxton and Lindsay Hassett. John Major's favourite, Denis Compton, is surrounded by the similarly flamboyantly gifted Keith Miller and England and Middlesex sidekick Bill Edrich.

Godfrey Evans is preceded by Les Ames in the wicketkeeping pantheon, and succeeded by his less demonstrative competitors for the England gloves, Keith Andrew and Arthur McIntyre, and international rivals Gil Langley of Australia and the Springbok John Waite. Members of the Surrey teams who won the county championship in seven successive seasons in the 1950s are grouped together (the Bedser twins, Peter Loader, Tony Lock and the two captains, Stuart Surridge and Peter May); so, too, are the leading lights in Hampshire's championship win of 1961 (strike bowlers Derek Shackleton and Butch White plus their inimitable captain, Colin Ingleby-Mackenzie). Colin Cowdrey is sandwiched between two more notable, spiritual cricketers in Dickie Dodds and David Sheppard, who was England captain and later Bishop of Liverpool. The Right Reverend Lord Sheppard of Liverpool also contributes a piece on Cowdrey, who, along with Compton, is one of only two players from the eighty-two included here to be accorded two entries; it probably helps that Compton has John Major and Michael Parkinson batting for him, and Cowdrey has Michael Henderson and the Bishop. Two of cricket's great writers and broadcasters, John Arlott and E.W. Swanton, are remembered affectionately by Tony Lewis and Scyld Berry, themselves two particularly perceptive journalists from the *Sunday Telegraph*. The book concludes with Parkinson's tribute to George Pope, the Derbyshire all-rounder, which defies the criteria set out above, but by hook and by crook is the last in this book because the resonant pay-off line feels just about perfect. 'He was,' Parkinson wrote, 'a master of his craft and not many of us will go to our graves with that as our epitaph.'

Garrison Keillor, the American writer, broadcaster and humorist, once quipped: 'They say such nice things about people at their funerals that it makes me sad to realise that I'm going to miss mine by just a few days.' So it goes with obituaries. Apart from Mark Twain and several other deaths 'greatly exaggerated' by premature notices, the subject never gets to read or hear what everyone thought of them. Keillor is still alive at the time of writing, and in these days of instant news and comment will miss his obit by a matter of hours. It has probably already been written: it lurks guarded by password somewhere in a hidden newspaper vault awaiting its moment on the public stage. But he certainly won't read it. Like the nice things people say at funerals, it will extol the virtues of his literary output, his radio shows, his fine upstanding character and include a few of his *pons mots* like the one above.

All the tributes contained in *The Promise of Endless Summer* follow the Garrison Keillor dictum of niceness; all, that is, bar one. Simon Hughes's piece soon after the death at forty-four of Sylvester Clarke is the exception to the rule. Flattering to the deceased it is not. Hughes had faced Surrey's hostile West Indian quickie, and barely lived to tell the tale. (Well, except in 690 words under the headline 'Nasty, brutish and short' in his *Telegraph* column some two decades later.) Hughes recalled that he was just two millimetres (the width of the Perspex side-piece on his helmet) from his own death notice after being clunked on the head by one of Clarke's most unpleasant deliveries. It provides a rare exposé from the middle of the pitch on how terrifying and dangerous cricket can sometimes be.

In contrast, and only a month earlier, Mark Nicholas penned a more affectionate tribute to another West Indian fast bowler. Nicholas was a team-mate, captain and friend of Malcolm Marshall during his fifteen summers in county cricket with Hampshire. 'If there was an element of ruthlessness about Marshall's bowling,' he wrote, 'there was not a hint of anything but warmth and generosity in his personality.' Maybe Nicholas was fortunate not to face Marshall anywhere other than in the nets, but even there he was renowned for passing on his infinite knowledge to friend and foe.

'If much of Malcolm characterised the calypso cricketer, much too epitomised the model professional,' Nicholas concluded.

One of the features of the *Telegraph*'s cricket coverage over the years has been its ability to call on former players to offer their insight into the game, and wax lyrical about old team-mates and opponents. Hughes and Nicholas are just two of them. David Green, the former Lancashire and Gloucestershire opener, has been a longtime *Telegraph* stalwart and was able to offer different asides upon the deaths of Arthur Milton and Derek Shackleton. Green recalled a match where Milton shielded him from the spinner who was tying him up in knots and enabled him to gain confidence from the comparative safety of the other end. He also revealed how Shackleton winkled him out in both innings for one of only two 'pairs' he suffered during his career. He remembered he was 'helpless both times'.

Derek Pringle, the sagacious incumbent cricket correspondent, dwells upon a catch he dropped in a Test match against the West Indies more than a quarter of a century ago. Graham Dilley had reduced the tourists to 54 for five and 'a rout looked likely until your correspondent spilled Gus Logie off him at first slip ... England lost, but it might have been very different had I not floored that catch'. Not that Dilley, who died in 2011 aged just fifty-two, held it against him; he was, wrote Pringle, 'probably too gentle to be the consummate fast bowler'. Fred Trueman would have raged; after all, he once admonished David Sheppard for the latest in a succession of dropped catches thus: 'It's a pity the Reverend don't put his hands together more often in the field.'

Pringle also paid tribute to that most popular of umpires, David Shepherd, whom he had played against when an undergraduate at Cambridge. He remembered the bruised knuckles suffered by the students for underestimating a man who may have looked like a toby jug but who hit the ball with all the power of a blacksmith. It was also during his university days that Pringle first encountered the tormented soul that was Peter Roebuck. He considered that the one-time Somerset captain possessed 'one of the keenest, most analytical minds of his generation', but does not seem overly surprised that he should die by his own hand. Michael Parkinson, in contrast, cannot get his head around David Bairstow's suicide. 'Why, old lad, why?', he asks.

Parkinson also wrote of Harold Larwood, Keith Miller and Denis Compton with the benefit of his own dealings with them. Larwood, Miller and Compton! Not a bad triumvirate with whom to discuss some of the key moments in cricket history. When he met Larwood over a convivial lunch with other luminaries, the 'B' word, he says, 'ticked away in the corner of the room like an unexploded bomb'. Jack Fingleton, the old Australian batsman, almost set it off by suggesting Larwood was too good a bowler to need to resort to Bodyline tactics in the 1932–33 Ashes series. Larwood defused it by replying: 'I was merely following the instructions of my captain.' Then, Parkinson reported, 'he produced from his jacket pocket a yellow duster and unfolded it to reveal a silver ash tray. The inscription said: "To a great bowler from a grateful captain. D.R. Jardine". The lettering was faint from nearly fifty years of spit and polish'. Parkinson said he did not believe Larwood was an unwitting accomplice in Jardine's plan to use 'fast leg-theory' to intimidate Don Bradman, but he was 'never likely to begin to fathom the undercurrents of intrigue created by his captain's strategy'. He paid the price for it and would never play for England again. But Parkinson's piece also tells how Larwood ended up living out his days 'in suburban Sydney amid the accents that once denounced him as the devil'.

Two obituaries you suspect Parkinson would have enjoyed retelling were the highly unorthodox 'Bomber' Wells and Frank Parr. Both appeared in the obituary columns with uncredited authors, but both articles are close to being masterpieces of the genre. Bryan Wells played for Gloucestershire and Nottinghamshire during the

1950s and 1960s and would bowl off one step if it was hot, two if it was cold, and none if he could get away with it. He once contrived to bowl an over while the cathedral clock at Worcester struck twelve. Wells was described as 'one of the most eccentric and funniest county cricketers' and his obituary does him credit. Parr, meanwhile, was Lancashire's wicketkeeper and was even close to selection for an England tour. A scruffy and laid-back individual, his career took an unusual turn and he ended up playing alongside George Melly as a trombonist in one of the more hedonistic jazz bands of the late 1950s. His obituary is juxtaposed here with that of Dickie Dodds, who dedicated his life to Moral Re-Armament.

In places, *The Promise of Endless Summer* picks up some of the themes of its 2011 predecessor, *Not In My Day, Sir*, the collection of cricket letters to the *Daily Telegraph*: of things being better in the good old days. It will therefore, hopefully, induce similar wry smiles of recognition. Like John Major and the *Telegraph*, cricket is essentially conservative in nature and has undergone major makeovers in recent times, and not always for the better. In *Not In My Day, Sir*, readers put forward their gripes and criticisms, some good-humouredly constructive, others harrumphingly withering. In this sister companion, readers will pick up on signs of those changes from the last sixty or seventy years. No more are there divisions between amateur and professional, gentleman and player, not least because there are no longer amateurs, and some might argue, no gentlemen, either. And no more do players routinely pass one thousand runs or one hundred wickets in a summer as they did back then: they don't play enough to get close, harrumph. Yet, as this book reveals, Derek Shackleton, for one, took a century of wickets in a season *twenty* times in his career. And we have already learnt that Compton and Edrich both topped *three* thousand runs in 1947 while playing *for the same teams*. Oh, for those heady days again!

But then maybe they never really go away, at least not in spirit. As John Major put it in another context two decades ago, in fifty years' time Britain 'will still be the country of long shadows on county grounds, warm beer, invincible green suburbs, dog lovers and pools fillers'. And maybe skipping across the outfield of some county ground during the tea interval there will be a small boy (or, indeed, girl) destined to become prime minister who has been watching a cricketer who has caught his or her imagination. And maybe, in fifty or sixty years' time, he or she will sit down beneath the hustings and compose an appreciation of that player. Who is that inspirational player now in our midst? Perhaps it will be someone, from either side, who performs heroically in the two Ashes series of 2013: the heirs of Bradman, Compton, Miller and Edrich.

This collection of tributes to the heroes of the past was the brainchild of publisher and cricket connoisseur Graham Coster, who commissioned it for Aurum, and whose interest has spurred the project along. My thanks go then, initially, to him; and also to Caroline Buckland, head of books and entertainment at Telegraph Media Group, for supporting Graham's enthusiasm; to my hard-working editor Melissa Smith; to the ever-helpful Gavin Fuller, Lorraine Goodspeed and the rest of the staff in the *Telegraph* library for facilitating my research; to my invaluable former colleague Andrew Baker for his advice and kind words; to the writers, bylined and otherwise, prime ministers included, who have written so vividly about the outstanding cricketers contained within; and to the various editors who found space to accommodate them in the newspaper.

MARTIN SMITH
November 2012

The Promise of Endless Summer

Michael Colin Cowdrey grew up batting at the St Lawrence Ground in Canterbury in the 1950s, so he knew all about the Elysian Fields as a young man. Now that he has passed away, he can join the ghosts of other run-stealers as they flicker to and fro. For those of a certain age, Cowdrey's cover drive, recollected through the haze of an August afternoon, was more than a thing of beauty. It was, and it remains, a stroke to unlock the memory; a memory, intangible yet always present, of the game as it was and as it can be, like some promise of endless summer.

Michael Henderson on Colin Cowdrey

5 MARCH 2001
DON BRADMAN
Chilled by the Great Man's
Remorseless Style
W.F. Deedes

To watch any innings by Bradman was rewarding, but those of us who saw him batting in 1930 probably had the best of it. For that was the year he struck international cricket like a whirlwind, dominating the Test matches here in a style no other cricketer has matched. From the time of his first Sheffield Shield match for New South Wales in 1927, when he scored 118, we had known there was a star on the horizon. But nobody was prepared for the manner in which he opened the season here in 1930 with a double century against Worcestershire, 185 not out against Leicestershire and 334 in the third Test at Headingley.

I watched most of his first innings in the second Test at Lord's, when he scored 254 not out of Australia's total of 729 for six declared. It would be fair to say that he was fortunate to come in at number three, after Woodfull and Ponsford, both of them scoring machines, had put on 162 for the first wicket. That stand ended, I remember, after a short break in play while both teams were presented to King George V in front of the pavilion. E.W. Swanton used to observe, such interludes often produced what he called a royal wicket. Woodfull, unmoved by the experience, went on to score 155. He and Bradman stayed together that day until almost the close of play. Against the

English bowlers, G.O. Allen, Maurice Tate, J.C. White and R.W.V. Robins, Bradman gave no semblance of a chance. Never have I witnessed in any sort of cricket, let alone a Test match, such complete mastery of bat over ball. Old hands will spot the fact that all our main bowlers except Tate were amateurs. I don't think that made any difference at all. They were the best we had. What undoubtedly counted in Bradman's favour was a benign Lord's wicket, which yielded sixteen hundred runs in the match, and Australia's enormous batting strength. After him came Kippax and McCabe.

But even those factors cannot dim the performance. Through my binoculars I could see from my seat in the Mound Stand some intent and solemn faces in the Lord's pavilion. They were watching a new force in the game. Bradman's supremacy, it struck me then and on other occasions I saw him bat, seemed to emanate from the speed with which he spotted what the ball was likely to do after it left the bowler's hand. All successful batsmen need a quick eye. Bradman's sight must have been phenomenal. There was a wonderfully unhurried tempo about his shot-making. He seemed always to have time to move his feet in a way that gave him maximum leverage against the ball. More than any other batsman I have watched, he always had time to shape the shot he wanted to play.

As well as that gift, he was extraordinarily fit, showing no signs of fatigue after the first or indeed the second century. Looking back, it was an innings I admired but did not much enjoy. At seventeen, I was more partisan than I am today. It was not pleasurable to see the best of English bowling treated with such contempt. I found Bradman's remorselessness on that sunny afternoon slightly chilling. I felt almost resentful of my kindly uncle, who had chosen this particular day for my treat at Lord's, and afterwards regretted missing K.S. Duleepsinhji's 173 in England's first innings and Percy Chapman's 121 in the second.

But it came as no great surprise to me when a few days later that July Bradman scored 334 at Leeds. 'I watched that chap,' I boasted to my friends, 'and we are up against it.' Better cricketing minds than mine were reaching the same conclusion. Their thinking paved the way for the notorious Bodyline series in Australia of 1932–33. Bradman in 1930 should be seen in the context of those times. It was the year after the Wall Street Crash. The Great Slump was upon us, and most people felt impoverished and depressed. No matter which side you were on, here was a star who cheered you up no end.

Donald George Bradman: b Cootamundra, New South Wales, 27 August 1908; d 25 February 2001

8 APRIL 1991
BILL PONSFORD
World Record-Breaking Batsman
E.W. Swanton

William Harold Ponsford was one of the most prolific scorers in cricket history and half of an ever-memorable opening partnership with W.M. Woodfull, his Victorian state and Test captain. Bill Ponsford announced himself as a twenty-two-year-old by breaking, in 1922–23, the record first-class score held for more than a quarter of a century by A.C. MacLaren, who had scored 424 for Lancashire against Somerset at Taunton in 1895. He made 429 out of Victoria's world record of 1,059 on the great Melbourne Oval against a modest Tasmanian side. The next year he took part in the highest Australian partnership (as it still is) of 456, also at Melbourne, against Queensland. When Victoria beat their own previous best with the still pre-eminent 1,107 against New South Wales in 1926–27, Ponsford made 334 of his score of 352 in a day, Melbourne once again being the venue. By this time, he had made 110 not out against England in his first Test and 128, on his home pitch, in his next.

A youngster eight years his junior was, however, taking due note in the country at Bowral, New South Wales – D.G. Bradman by name. Two seasons after his debut, Bradman bettered the world record by notching 452 not out against the luckless Queenslanders. Then came Bradman's all-conquering tour of England in 1930, with Ponsford a valuable member of the supporting cast. Thereafter,

Bradman's triumphal career proceeded with scarcely a hitch for, whereas his technique was almost proof against mortal error, Ponsford was fallible against speed – especially Larwood's. Ponsford, in fact, was dropped from the Test side in the 1932–33 Bodyline series, only to reappear and average ninety-four against England in 1934. Thereupon, before his thirty-fourth birthday, he announced his retirement.

Woodfull and Ponsford were a contrast at the crease, the former, with the minimum of back lift, generally a phlegmatic wearer-down, while Ponsford was always prepared to take the battle to the enemy. Bradman dominated his day, averaging ninety-five over his career. Yet only two other Australians in history, Ponsford and Woodfull, have boasted a career average in the sixties. Ponsford made 13,819, including forty-seven hundreds, at 65.18. The figures behind the decimal point are the measure of his advantage over his old friend, Billy Woodfull, who finished with 65.00.

William Harold Ponsford: b Fitzroy North, Victoria, 19 October 1900; d 6 April 1991

8 APRIL 1986
SYDNEY COPLEY
Catches Win Matches
E.W. Swanton

Sydney Herbert Copley was the Nottinghamshire ground staff cricketer whose catch when fielding substitute turned the Trent Bridge Test match of 1930 between England and Australia. On the last day England had to take the field without Harold Larwood, who had gone down with gastritis, and Copley was brought on in his place. Against the weakened attack Bradman and McCabe had made a brisk 77 together for the fourth wicket when McCabe was brilliantly caught off Tate's bowling inches above the ground at deep mid-on by Copley, diving to his right and rolling over. From that point, all went England's way, Chapman leading them to his sixth successive victory over Australia.

Sydney Herbert Copley: b Hucknall, Nottinghamshire, 1 November 1905; d 1 April 1986

7 OCTOBER 1992
BILL O'REILLY
The Tiger Who was Never Tamed
E.W. Swanton

Bill O'Reilly was an Australian cricketer of imperishable memory. In the 1930s he stood clear above all of his type. His fame rests on his appearance in only twenty-seven Test matches, for he was twenty-six before he won his first cap and his skills were at their height when War came. He played one Test in New Zealand afterwards, but decided that at the age of forty his legs could scarcely sustain his large, lumbering frame on hard Australian pitches and retired to the press box. O'Reilly's pungent opinions enlivened the sports pages of the *Sydney Morning Herald* for more than forty years. To describe his critical style as trenchant would be an understatement. When Kerry Packer attempted his takeover of world cricket in 1977 he found an implacable opponent in his fellow Sydney-sider. One-day cricket as played Down Under, with the coloured clothing and all the commercial ballyhoo attending it, was anathema to O'Reilly. While some temporised, he saw that the primary object of the true game, to bowl out the other side, was being perverted into that of stopping them scoring.

Bill O'Reilly's name is inevitably closely linked with that of Sir Donald Bradman since before they came together into the state team they had been antagonists playing as country boys for their townships. When O'Reilly, a twenty-year-old at a teacher-training college, first played for Wingello at Bowral in 1926, Bradman, three years his junior and already the local prodigy, scored 234 not out. O'Reilly could only console himself that he had had the boy wonder missed at slip and that he had bowled him first ball when the game was continued the following weekend. From this cricket they both graduated in the Australian manner via Sydney clubs to the New South Wales XI.

Though O'Reilly was already a prolific wicket-taker his advance was much the slower, probably because the highly individual plunging action, front-on and knees bent, did not commend itself to the purists. Ian Peebles called it 'a glorious rampage of flailing arms and legs', from which emerged at a full slow-medium pace, and sometimes faster, every ball in a wrist-spinner's armoury, delivered with a rare degree of accuracy and an unusually high bounce. It was delivered, too, with a malignity of facial expression which inspired the nickname of 'the Tiger'. The genial side of his nature was well to the fore off the field. But on it he was a figure of rare hostility.

O'Reilly was effective on any surface, for he seemed able always to induce those extra inches of bounce which made for such a rigorous examination in judgment of length and footwork. Even on the super-placid Oval pitch of 1938 on which Hutton made his record 364 and England declared at 903 for seven, he bowled eighty-five overs, conceding just two runs an over for three of the best wickets. His comments on that pitch remain splendidly lurid. On another pitch of consummate ease at Old Trafford in 1934 he had the wickets of Walters, Wyatt and Hammond in four balls, the last two clean bowled, and finished with seven for 189 out of a total of 627 for nine. When O'Reilly found a responsive English pitch – as at Trent Bridge in 1934 and Headingley in 1938 – he was too much even for the best. In the Headingley match his ten for 122 combined with Bradman's third successive Test hundred on the ground to seal Australia's grip on the Ashes.

William Joseph O'Reilly: b White Cliffs, New South Wales, 20 December 1905; d 6 October 1992

22 APRIL 1995

R.E.S. WYATT

England Captain with
a Bulldog Spirit

R.E.S. Wyatt was England's senior Test captain for many years, a patriarch whose achievement over a playing career lasting nearly thirty years has been bettered only by a handful. Wyatt's appointment to lead England in the Ashes-deciding fifth Test against Australia at the Oval in 1930 – in place of the popular and successful A.P.F. Chapman – was a sensation comparable in those days only to the dropping of A.W. Carr in favour of Chapman against Australia four years earlier. Chapman's promotion had brought success. Wyatt's did not – though small blame can be attached to him.

He led England, soundly if without inspiration, fifteen times in his forty Test appearances, including the 1934 home series against Australia, M.C.C.'s tour of the West Indies in 1934–35 and South Africa's visit to England in 1935. He was vice-captain to D.R. Jardine in Australia in 1932–33 and G.O. Allen there in 1936–37, fulfilling both roles to general satisfaction. The first was especially taxing, in that he strongly opposed the Bodyline tactics.

Robert Elliott Storey Wyatt was a scion of the Wyatt architectural dynasty and a cousin of the future Lord Wyatt of Weeford. He played for Warwickshire from 1923, with little impact at first. But he persevered, improving gradually until a successful M.C.C. tour to India in 1926–27 promised greater things. The next winter he toured South Africa with M.C.C. and, after beginning his Test career with a duck, held his England place in a drawn series. Against South Africa at Old Trafford in 1929 Wyatt made the first post-War Test hundred by an amateur, and over the next decade established himself as one of the most dependable batsmen in England, with periodic effectiveness as a medium-pace change bowler.

In 1934 he succeeded Jardine as captain on the latter's retirement. Though England were thwarted by the brilliance of Bradman and the spin partnership of O'Reilly and Grimmett, Wyatt had the satisfaction (thanks to a thunderstorm and Hedley Verity's bowling) of leading England to what remains the only victory over Australia at Lord's since 1896.

Wyatt was all of a piece, bulldog in looks and spirit, his cricket a perfect reflection of the man. In mid-March 1935, in the Jamaica Test match, a fast ball from Martindale lifted and fractured his jaw in four places with a noise like a rifle shot. When he recovered consciousness Bob called for pen and paper and wrote that he attached no blame to the bowler. Before being wheeled off to hospital he also revised the batting order. Six weeks later, leading M.C.C. against Surrey at Lord's, he put himself in first and made a hundred. The next month he faced the fast South African attack at Trent Bridge and made 149, his highest score in Test cricket.

Wyatt took over the Warwickshire captaincy in 1930 and held it for eight years, at the end of which the committee – seeking a more zestful approach – announced the appointment of Peter Cranmer, the twenty-three-year-old captain of England at rugby football. The matter was not handled tactfully, though. Wyatt continued to play under Cranmer for the two remaining pre-War summers, but was deeply hurt. After the War he moved across the border to Worcestershire, where he had six happy summers, latterly as captain.

At Taunton in 1951, in the last week of his last season (and now past fifty), he faced the last ball of the match against Somerset with six runs needed to win; he duly drove it high into the pavilion for victory. Almost twenty years earlier he and C.F. Walters had made 160 together at Lord's in an opening partnership of an hour and a half, which brought the Gentlemen, under his leadership, to their first victory over the Players since the First World War.

Robert Elliott Storey Wyatt: b Milford Heath House, Surrey, 2 May 1901; d 20 April 1995

24 JULY 1995
HAROLD LARWOOD
The Master Who Paid a Heavy Price
for His Greatness
Michael Parkinson

Long before I met him I knew him well. My father told me he was the greatest fast bowler that ever drew breath and paid him the ultimate compliment of hero worship by copying his run to the wicket. Jack Fingleton, who also knew what he was talking about, said he was the best fast bowler he faced. He was, said Fingo, 'the master'. Harold Larwood was a giant in my imagination, a legendary figure whose bowling frightened the greatest batsman there has ever been (and a few more besides) and in doing so created a political brouhaha of such resonance it echoes still, sixty years on.

When I first saw him standing outside a Sydney restaurant in 1979, he looked like one of the miners who would loiter around the pubs on Sunday mornings waiting for the doors to open at mid-day. He seemed uncomfortable in his suit as if it was his Sunday best, his trilby hat was at a jaunty angle and he was smoking a cigarette which he cupped in the palm of his hand as if shielding it from a wind. He was medium height with good shoulders and the strong, square hands of someone who had done some shovelling in his life as well as bowling. My father, in heaven at the time, would have been delighted with my impression that he and his great hero were peas from the same pod.

On the other hand, I had expected something altogether more substantial, someone more in keeping with the image I had of a man who terrorised opponents and whose fearsome reputation was such that at one moment in time governments were in thrall as he ran in to bowl. In all of sport there never was a story to match the Bodyline saga. At its heart was the ultimate sporting challenge: a contest between the two greatest players in the world. In 1932–33, Donald Bradman was in his prime, the finest batsman of his generation, or any other before or since. Harold Larwood was also in his pomp, the fastest bowler in the world and about to prove himself the most lethal and unerring there has ever been. The impresario of this world title contest was Douglas Jardine, the captain of England, patrician, implacable and a terrible snob who treated Australians with a contempt he never bothered to conceal. The story that unfolded around these three characters had everything except sex and a happy ending. I was tempted to say it would have made a marvellous soap for television, except one was produced and a right mess they made of it.

The controversy stirred by Bodyline pursued Harold Larwood all his days. It changed him from a cricketer into a hunted man who hid away in a sweet shop in Blackpool before being persuaded by Jack Fingleton to seek a new life in Australia, where he ended his days surrounded by his large family in suburban Sydney amid the accents that once denounced him as the devil. It was Jack Fingleton and Keith Miller who arranged my meeting with Harold; Bill O'Reilly was there, too; and Arthur Morris and Ray Lindwall, so you could say I was in the best of company. There were so many questions I wanted to ask but dare not unless I turned what was a friendly lunch into a press conference. In any case, in that company I was superfluous to requirements except as a witness to what happened.

We sat at a round table on a spring day in Sydney. We all drank wine except Harold who said he was a beer man. 'Always had a pint when I was bowling,' he said. 'We used to sneak it on with the soft drinks. A pint for me and one for Bill Voce. You must put back what you sweat out,' he said. 'I hope you weren't drunk when you bowled at me,' said Jack Fingleton. 'I didn't need any inspiration to get you out,' Harold Larwood replied. Jack said of all the bowlers he faced Larwood was the fastest and had the best control. 'He was a very great bowler. Used to skid the bouncer. Throat ball,' said Jack. Larwood took the compliment and said: 'You might not have been the best batsman I bowled against but you were certainly the bravest. I could hit you all right but you wouldn't go down. You weren't frightened, not like one or two I could mention but won't,' he said.

Tiger O'Reilly said he was once sent out to bat against Harold when the ball was flying about, having been instructed by his skipper to stay at the crease at all costs. He was endeavouring to follow these instructions, and was halfway through his backlift when Larwood bowled him a ball he sensed but did not see. 'I felt the draught as it went by and heard it hit Duckworth's gloves,' said Tiger. Being a sensible fellow he decided on a new method which, as he described it, involved him standing alongside the square leg umpire with his bat stretched towards the stumps. 'It was from this position,' said Tiger, 'I was perfectly placed to observe a most extraordinary occurrence. Larwood bowled me a ball of such pace and ferocity that it struck the off bail and reduced it to a small pile of sawdust.' When I first told this story a reader wrote to say that what O'Reilly claimed was clearly impossible. I wrote back informing the reader that O'Reilly was Irish and heard nothing more on the matter.

Jack Fingleton told Harold Larwood: 'You didn't need to bowl Bodyline. You were a good enough bowler to get anyone out by normal methods.' It was the first time during our luncheon that anyone had mentioned 'Bodyline'. Until then, the word had ticked away in the corner of the room like an unexploded bomb. Harold smiled. 'I was merely following the instructions of my captain,' he said. He produced from his jacket pocket a yellow duster and unfolded it to reveal a silver ash tray. The inscription said: 'To a great bowler from a grateful captain. D.R. Jardine'. The lettering was faint from nearly fifty years of spit and polish.

Jardine was the Field Marshal of Bodyline, Larwood his secret weapon. Jardine was the strategist, Larwood the assassin. I think it wrong to portray Larwood as the unwitting accomplice as some have done. It underestimates his strength of character, denies his intelligence and, most of all, does not take into account his determination to show Bradman and the rest of the Aussies who the boss really was. But whereas Jardine fully understood the consequences of what he planned, Larwood was never likely to begin to fathom the undercurrents of intrigue created by his captain's strategy. They did for him in the end.

At our lunch, Harold recalled the day in 1933 when an Australian supporter accosted him and said: 'I hope you never play cricket again.' Harold Larwood replied: 'How dare you say that when cricket is my life, my job, my livelihood.' It wasn't too long before his critic's wish was granted and Harold Larwood, who thought he had been playing cricket for a living, wondered if he might have been mistaken.

After Jardine's team had thrashed the Australians, Harold Larwood, who was injured, went home ahead of the main party. He told me he realised he was to be made the scapegoat when he arrived in London to be confronted by a mob of journalists without any help from the M.C.C., who left him to his own devices. Before reaching London, after his ship docked in France, Larwood had been joined by his Nottinghamshire captain, A.W. Carr, whom he took to be his official escort. Carr quizzed him about events in Australia which Larwood answered candidly as he would to his skipper. It was only when they arrived in London and Harold found himself on his own that he realised Carr had been working for a newspaper.

Harold said he arrived in Nottingham by train in angry mood in the early hours of the morning, to be greeted with a brass band and a hero's welcome. Ordinary cricket lovers had no time for the political arguments taking place between the governments of Great Britain and Australia. All they cared about was England bringing home the Ashes and, as far as they were concerned, the man who did the job was Harold Larwood. He enjoyed his celebrity for a while and capitalised on it. There was talk of making a movie and he went to Gamages store in London for a week to demonstrate Bodyline bowling to an admiring public. For the week of personal appearances he earned five times more than he was paid for the entire tour of Australia. He told us that the worst moment came when he was asked to apologise for the way he had bowled. He refused. 'I had nothing to be ashamed about,' he said. He never played for England again and he had only a few more seasons with Notts. Disenchanted, he bought a shop in Blackpool and didn't even put his name above the door in case it attracted rubber-neckers.

It was here that Jack Fingleton found him in 1948 and persuaded him to emigrate. Jack, who also worked as a parliamentary reporter and knew his way around the corridors of power, pulled a few strings and arranged that the prime minister of Australia, Ben Chifley, be on hand to greet Harold when he arrived. Mr Chifley was a dinki-di Aussie with an ocker accent. After introducing the two men, Jack left them to have a natter. Ten minutes later, he was joined by the prime minister. 'He's a nice bloke but I can't understand a word he's saying,' he said to Jack. Ten minutes later, Larwood appeared. 'It was nice of the prime minister to see me, but I wish I knew what he was on about,' said Harold. So Jack Fingleton sometimes interpreted for two men who both thought they were speaking English.

Harold laughed as Jack told the tale. 'And I still haven't lost my accent,' he said. And he hadn't. 'Coming to Australia was the best thing that happened to me. I've been very happy here. I was signing in at a golf club some time ago and came to the bit where they ask you where you come from and my friend suggested I put Nottingham down in the book. I told him my home was in Sydney and pointed out I had lived in Australia longer than their best fast bowler, Dennis Lillee.'

We lunched together twice more before he became housebound because of his blindness. I called to congratulate him on being awarded the M.B.E. in 1993. I didn't tell him it was sixty years overdue. Like elephants, the Establishment have long memories and small brains. With Harold gone, only Bradman remains of the key protagonists in the Bodyline story. Neither man has told the whole truth, choosing to keep to themselves what they really thought about each other. In that sense, the story has no ending and both men will be remembered for what we don't know about them as they will for their deeds on the field of play. Between them, the Boy from Bowral and the Lad from Nuncargate played out a story that will forever interest lovers of cricket and social historians looking for clues about the attitudes and mores of that time.

I was lucky to meet Harold Larwood and treasure the memory. I never saw him bowl, but my father did and Jack Fingleton, too. I think Jack should have the last word. 'One could tell his art by his run to the wicket. It was a poem of athletic grace, as each muscle gave over to the other with perfect balance and the utmost power. I will never see a greater fast bowler than Larwood, I am sure of that. He was the master.'

**Harold Larwood: b Nuncargate, Nottinghamshire,
14 November 1904; d 22 July 1995**

7 JUNE 1984
BILL VOCE
The Prince of Bowlers
E.W. Swanton

The name of Bill Voce, one of the best of all left-arm fast bowlers, will be associated for ever in history with that of his great partner for Nottinghamshire and England, Harold Larwood. Together they had the chief part in winning the county championship of 1929; together, under the stern instruction of their captain, D.R. Jardine, they perfected in the 1932–33 Test series in Australia the fast leg-theory attack which came to be known as Bodyline. Larwood so injured his left foot on that tour that he could never again recapture anything approaching his phenomenal speed, though he soldiered on for several more seasons of county cricket at fast-medium pace in company with Voce, his junior by five years. Both before and after the Bodyline tour the Nottinghamshire bowling, on the orders of the captain, A.W. Carr, sometimes overstepped the margin of fair play, and it was not until Nottinghamshire put the leadership into more acceptable hands that relations with several of the counties were repaired.

Happily, too, though Larwood's Test days were past, the breach with Lord's that had prevented Voce's selection for England for four of his prime years was healed, and he sailed for Australia again with G.O. Allen's team for the 1936–37 tour. With twenty-six wickets at 21 runs each he headed England's Test bowling averages, and such was the paucity of talent after the Second World War that in his thirty-eighth year, he made a third tour to Australia in 1946–47. The spirit still was as willing as ever but of the fire and elasticity of that bounding run and classical delivery only spasmodic vestiges remained.

Voce, as a tall, slim lad, walked from the colliery town of Bucknall to Trent Bridge in the late 1920s in search of a trial. There his natural talent was at once recognised. He had a long, loose arm and a natural flowing action, with the ability, bowling over the wicket, to swing the ball either way in the air. After the shine had gone, now round the wicket, he straightened the ball still at lively speed, unless the conditions suggested slow-medium spin. He was indeed an artist and an athlete quite out of the ordinary.

William Voce: b Annesley Woodhouse, Nottinghamshire, 8 August 1909; d 6 June 1984

7 SEPTEMBER 1987
BILL BOWES
Finest Opening County Bowler
of His Generation

E.W. Swanton

Bill Bowes's name will be always associated with that of Hedley Verity: a sufficiency of speed at one end, of spin at the other, and artistry and guile at both. Though born in the heart of the West Riding, Bowes came to first-class cricket not through the Yorkshire system but as a member of the Lord's staff, which he joined in answer to an advertisement. Elderly M.C.C. members may recall a very tall, somewhat shambling youth looking anything but a budding bowler wearing *pince-nez* secured to his ear by a chain. Bowes first came to notice by taking a hat-trick against Cambridge in his second first-class match. Yorkshire soon claimed their own, M.C.C. releasing him from a nine-year contract.

From 1931 to 1939 Bowes took one hundred wickets a season, soon subordinating sheer pace and an over-emphasis on the bouncer in favour of skilful use of the seam. He bowled from a height of six feet four inches with an arm at full upward stretch, generally to a full length with a late outswing and life and lift on almost any pitch. Under Brian Sellars's tight leadership, with Verity in support and nowt given away in the field, Bowes was the finest county opening bowler of his generation. In the field his mobility was modest, and as a batsman, though dogged at a pinch, he goes down in history as one of the few who have taken more wickets (1,639 at 17 apiece) than they have made runs (1,530, average eight).

In the winter of 1932–33 Bowes went to Australia as the fourth fast bowler on what became the 'Bodyline tour', and is remembered for bowling Bradman for a duck first ball at Melbourne when The Don dragged the expected bouncer on to his stumps. That was Bowes's only wicket and his only Test of the series. Very much a bowler for English conditions, Bowes took sixty-eight Test wickets at 22 runs a time – an economical rate considering he saw so much of Bradman, whose wicket he took four times more, albeit after he had made big scores.

At the age of forty Bowes settled down to a long career of cricket writing. He was an acknowledged authority on bowling theory and in much demand as a coach. His dry humour enlivened many a press box, and as a member of the Magic Circle he could occasionally be induced to surprise his friends with his skill as a conjuror.

**William Eric Bowes: b Elland, Yorkshire,
25 July 1908; d 4 September 1987**

30 DECEMBER 2006
NORMAN MITCHELL-INNES
Graceful Batsman Beset by Hay Fever

Norman Mitchell-Innes played for England against South Africa in 1935 when he was an Oxford undergraduate. In an era of gifted amateurs, 'Mandy' Mitchell-Innes stood out for the effortlessness of his timing and the grace of his technique, the kind of batsman who had only to lean on the ball to send it scudding to the boundary. Over his four seasons at Oxford (1934–37) he set a record with 3,319 runs for the university at an average of 47.41. No one – not the Nawab of Pataudi (senior or junior), not Colin Cowdrey, M.J.K. Smith, nor Abbas Ali Baig – has scored so highly for the university.

In May 1935 Mitchell-Innes caught Plum Warner's eye with a magnificent 168 for Oxford against the touring South Africans, and was chosen for the first Test at Trent Bridge. The England batting order for that match read Sutcliffe, Wyatt, Hammond, Mitchell-Innes, Leyland and Ames. Alas, Mitchell-Innes played back when he should have played forward and was lbw to Bruce Mitchell for only five. The selectors retained Mitchell-Innes for the next Test, at Lord's, but he felt he had to cry off because he was suffering from hay fever. 'I might be sneezing just as a catch came in the slips,' he wrote to Plum Warner. His friend Errol Holmes, with whom he was staying, took his place at Lord's while he went south of the river to the Oval and scored a brilliant century for Oxford against Surrey. He would never have another chance for England.

**Norman Stewart Mitchell-Innes: b Calcutta,
7 September 1914; d 28 December 2006**

20 JUNE 2005
SYED MUSHTAQ ALI
Indian Batsman of Grace and Flair

Syed Mushtaq Ali was a right-handed batsman of brilliance, flair and a loose, easy grace; at Old Trafford in 1936 he earned a niche in cricketing history by becoming the first Indian to score a Test century on foreign soil. As an opener who liked to attack the ball, Mushtaq thought nothing of using his feet to come down the wicket to the quick bowlers: 'We learnt to play fast bowling by practising on matting wickets,' he once recalled. 'We did not have helmets, and footwork was the key.'

Not immune to sudden rushes of blood to the head, Mushtaq was liable to jump out of the crease and hoist the ball straight into the hands of a fielder. Vijay Merchant, with whom he formed a brief but fruitful opening partnership, sometimes found himself alarmed by his team-mate's cavalier tendency to chase the bowling in the early overs of an innings. But Mushtaq could be particularly devastating with the hook shot, and he was adept at steering a ball pitched on the off side to on – a device which, he said, 'puzzled the opposition'. The Australian fast bowler Sam Loxton once speculated that Mushtaq could be the best opening batsman in the world.

On the face of it, Mushtaq's performance during the tour of England in 1936 was nothing special: he made a total of 1,078 runs, including four centuries, at an average of 25.06. But he did forge a strong opening partnership with Merchant. Opening in the first innings of the second Test at Old Trafford, he was run out for 13 in a freak fashion: Merchant drove a ball which struck Mushtaq's bat and rebounded to Arthur Fagg at mid-on – and Fagg threw down the bowler's wicket. In the second innings, the pair came out to bat with India facing a first-innings deficit of 368 and almost certain defeat. By stumps, they had put on 190 without loss. Already that day England had scored 398 runs, and the aggregate of 588 represented the highest number of runs scored on a single day in a Test match. Mushtaq – facing the likes of Gubby Allen, Alf Gover and Hedley Verity – went on to make 112 in a partnership of 203, helping to save the match for the tourists.

In pre-independence India his century was viewed as a national triumph. Sixty-eight years later, in 2004, it was voted eighteenth in a list of the all-time greatest hundreds in a poll conducted by *Wisden Asia Cricket*. Mushtaq's partnership with Merchant lasted for only four Test matches, but over those seven innings their average as an opening pair was 83.40. His final Test, against England at Madras, was in February 1952. India won by an innings and eight runs to draw the series, Mushtaq contributing 22. The match was notable for Vinoo Mankad's bowling figures of twelve for 108, and for being India's first Test victory.

Syed Mushtaq Ali: b Indore, 17 December 1914; d 18 June 2005

13 JANUARY 2000
H.D. READ
England's Fastest Bowler in 1935

H.D. 'Hopper' Read made a sensational impact as a fast bowler in the mid-1930s, not so much hopping as exploding on to the scene in his first match for Essex at Brentwood. The opposition were Surrey, for whom Jack Hobbs, then (in 1934) aged fifty-one, was making one of his last appearances. The story goes that Frank Woolley had told him the match offered a good opportunity of bringing his total of centuries (at 197) nearer the magic 200 mark. After all, in the previous match at Brentwood, Kent had declared at 803 for four.

But, faced with the responsibility of producing two three-day pitches on a club 'square', the groundsman had resorted to liquid manure. For the second match the mixture had not dried out. Read, bowling at a high pace, with a stiff wind at his back, removed Hobbs's cap with his first ball, and bowled him with his sixth. Surrey were dismissed in an hour and a half for 115, Read finishing with seven wickets for 35 runs. Essex won by an innings and 192 runs – oddly enough the same margin by which Kent had beaten them in the first match of this inaugural 'Week' at Brentwood.

After that, Read played whenever he was available. In 1935 he and M.S. Nichols bowled out an all-conquering Yorkshire side for 31 and 99 to give Essex their first victory over the White Rose since

1911. Read went on to play for England, though he had failed to get into his school side.

With Larwood's fast bowling days being over, Read in 1935 was rated the fastest bowler in England and the selectors, looking for victory to square the series, picked him for the fifth Test against South Africa. Read took six for 200 in the match and South Africa had little difficulty in achieving the draw that gave them success in the rubber. But his first-class career was brief: he toured Australia and New Zealand with M.C.C. that year and took eleven wickets for 100 runs in the first of four unofficial Tests. But on returning home he pursued his profession as an accountant.

Holcombe Douglas Read: b Woodford Green, Essex, 28 January 1910; d 5 January 2000

2 APRIL 2010
RON HAMENCE
The More Than Useful Travelling Reserve

Ron Hamence was a member of Don Bradman's 'invincible' touring team who swept triumphantly through England in 1948. He was a capable batsman, short in stature but nimble in his footwork against slow bowling, and eager to play strokes off the back foot when facing the fast men. On the tour of 1948, however, he did not make the Test side. He, Colin McCool and Doug Ring derided themselves as 'the ground staff', who turned out only when the stars of the side were rested for county games.

Having played with Bradman for South Australia since before the War, Hamence could get away with remarks to The Don that no one else in the side would have dared to venture. On the voyage to England he indulged in late-night singing with Lindsay Hassett and Doug Ring in the cabin next to the captain's; Hamence alone, however, dared to shout out: 'What did you think of that one, Braddles?' at the end of one of the songs. Bradman, for his part, was fond of Hamence, to whom he gave an excellent end-of-tour report in *Farewell to Cricket* (1950). 'He always batted well,' wrote The Don, 'and often at a critical moment made valuable runs. He was an extremely useful reserve who could have been played in the Tests with confidence. Above all he was a great tourist who did wonders for the morale of the side.' Hamence's figures for the tour – 582 runs at an average of 32.55 – only partly bear out this encomium. It was a measure of his popularity that his team-mates were as disappointed as he when he was stumped against Somerset at Taunton within a run of a century.

In later years he took a dim view of the dress and behaviour of modern players, remembering how Bradman expected his players to come down to breakfast in a suit. As for sledging: 'Bradman would not have allowed it.' His underlying reverence for his erstwhile captain frequently surfaced. 'If they'd televised one-day cricket when Bradman was in his prime,' he observed, 'I don't think the cameramen would have been quick enough to follow his shots. He was phenomenal.'

Ronald Arthur Hamence: b Hindmarsh, South Australia, 25 November 1915; d 24 March 2010

13 MAY 2003
ERNIE TOSHACK
Bradman's Favourite
Change Bowler

The Australian Ernie Toshack was a tall left-arm bowler of infinite variety and some peculiarity. Toshack's stock delivery was medium-pace over the wicket; unlike the general run of left-armers, however, he would cut the ball back from a right-hand batsman's off side to his leg. Yet he could also spin the ball conventionally from leg to off, bowl a faster one that went straight through, and occasionally drift one in the air either to off or to leg. His accuracy made him exceedingly difficult to score off when bowling to a defensive leg-side field. For this reason he was much prized in the years after the War by Don Bradman, who needed someone to pin down one end while his fast bowlers, Ray Lindwall and Keith Miller, were taking a rest. Yet Toshack's Test career was crammed into just twenty-nine months, from March 1946 to July 1948, when his left knee, always suspect, broke down in the fourth Test against England at Headingley. In his twelve Tests, he took forty-seven wickets at 21.04 each, and never played in a losing Australian side.

The visit of M.C.C. to Australia in 1946–47 was supposed to celebrate Commonwealth harmony in the aftermath of War; in fact it resulted in a fractious Test series, not least because there was little cordiality between the captains, Walter Hammond and Bradman. Toshack played in all five Tests, doing especially well in the first match at Brisbane, when he profited from a sticky wicket to claim three for 17 and six for 82, ensuring England's defeat by an innings and 332 runs. Hammond, alone among the English batsmen, showed the technique to cope with the conditions, but Toshack got him out in both innings. Next season, 1947–48, the Indians toured Australia, and in the first Test Toshack was able to take advantage of another sticky wicket at Brisbane to return figures of five wickets for two runs – achieved in only two overs and three balls – in the first innings, and then six for 29 in the second. His knee began to play up in that series, but he was now regarded as so crucial to Australia's attack that, after he had undergone a medical, the selectors decided to risk him on the tour of England in 1948.

Toshack was popular in England, alike for his dry humour and his tough-guy good looks. Team-mates christened him 'the Black Prince' and 'the film star', while crowds relished his loud "Ow whizz 'e?' appeals. Off the field he liked to play up to the natives, adopting a bowler hat, a tightly rolled umbrella and large cigars. He enjoyed some success as a player, too, though the advent of another left-arm bowler, Bill Johnston, made him rather less important than had originally been envisaged. Against M.C.C. at Lord's he won a long battle with Denis Compton, finishing with an analysis of six for 51.

There was plenty of work for him in the Tests, 128.1 overs in the first three matches, before his cartilage finally gave way. Toshack's best performance in that series was at Lord's where his five wickets in England's second innings set the seal on Australia's victory by 409 runs. Though his eleven victims in the series were relatively dearly bought, he had done precisely the job which Bradman demanded. And as a bonus he averaged 51 with the bat at number eleven, England's bowlers only once prising him out.

Ernest Raymond Herbert Toshack: b Cobar, New South Wales, 8 December 1914; d 11 May 2003

25 JUNE 1996
RAY LINDWALL
Fast Bowler with a
Well-Stocked Armoury

Ray Lindwall was arguably the greatest of all fast bowlers. At once graceful and menacing, Lindwall was able to send down an over of six very different balls with perfect disguise. This frightening ability derived from an exemplary action with a run-up so smooth that he gave the impression of being pulled on wheels by a wire. Rhythmically gathering pace into his leaping delivery stride, and with a classic sideways action, Lindwall in full flow made for a thrilling spectacle. When he bowled the first ball in a Test match anywhere in the world, the tension around the ground was electric as the batsman attempted to anticipate the outswinger, the inswinger, the bumper, the savage break-back, the slower ball, the even-faster-than-usual ball or one of his various cutters.

He took exactly half his Test wickets for Australia against England, and it was in this country that his skill bloomed most fully. Lindwall relished the damper atmosphere of Britain which gave the ball more chance to swing. This was particularly evident in 1948, when, in concert with Keith Miller, he produced some devastating performances. Despite his gentlemanly attitude, Lindwall landed six Englishmen in hospital during the course of that summer. His bumper was a fearsome weapon but sparingly used; forty-three of his eighty-six victims on that tour were clean bowled. He was, said Alec Bedser, a fast bowler with a medium-pacer's precise control. Lindwall took 228 Test wickets in sixty-one matches, at 23 runs apiece; only four Australians, Lillee, Benaud, McKenzie and McDermott, have taken more Test wickets, all of them at an inferior average.

Ray Lindwall was a modest man who once said: 'If you believe only half of what you read about me, I must have been a miraculous player, and I wasn't.' He could be somewhat bluff – as on the occasion during the 1948 tour, when Len Hutton asked Keith Miller to introduce him to Lindwall. Hutton had batted against him often but surprisingly they had never met off the pitch. Miller assured Hutton that Lindwall thought the world of him and encouraged the Yorkshireman to go over and talk to Lindwall, who was nearby. Hutton departed but returned moments later, looking downcast. Asked what had happened, Hutton reported: 'He said he was sick of the sight of me when I was batting against him and told me to bugger off.' 'Told you he admired you,' said Miller.

Raymond Russell Lindwall: b Mascot, New South Wales, 3 October 1921; d 23 June 1996

7 SEPTEMBER 1990
LEN HUTTON
An Exemplary Captain

England has lost one of its greatest cricketers with the death of Sir Leonard Hutton. A great entertainer and a technically superb bat, he was one of the brightest symbols of those gloomy years after the last War. Sir Len may have become a national hero through his feats on the field, but even to those who do not follow cricket he embodied sportsmanship, fine leadership and national pride. His 364 against the 1938 Australians, when he was barely twenty-two, has never been bettered by an Englishman in a Test, and only Sir Garfield Sobers has exceeded it. More significant, though, was Sir Len's appointment as England's first professional captain. Though there is cause to regret the extinction of the amateur, that appointment – and his success in it – was crucial to the process of making first-class cricket a professional game. He proved that exemplary captaincy could come from outside the officer class. It was for this, as much as for his batsmanship, that he received his knighthood.

Whatever his international success, Sir Len was first and foremost a Yorkshireman. The side he joined in the 1930s included Sutcliffe, Verity, Leyland and Bowes, and was perhaps the finest fielded by an English county. His contribution to Yorkshire's success during the two decades he played for it was immense, and it was fitting that he should have died its president. In the Three Ridings, his death will cause the greatest sorrow, made more poignant by awareness of the depths into which cricket there has since sunk; but it is a loss that all England shares with Yorkshire.

Leonard Hutton: b Fulneck, Pudsey, 23 June 1916; d 6 September 1990

30 APRIL 1999
CYRIL WASHBROOK
More Than Just Hutton's
Opening Partner

Cyril Washbrook, of Lancashire and England, was a cricketer of high quality in the years bestriding the Second World War, his name inseparable from that of his Test partner, Sir Leonard Hutton. In 1954 Washbrook became the first professional captain of Lancashire, a post he held with the utmost dignity at a time when most of the counties were still led by amateurs. It was the success in the job of such men as Washbrook, Dennis Brookes of Northamptonshire and Tom Dollery of Warwickshire that influenced the decision in the winter of 1962 to drop the distinction between amateurs and professionals.

Washbrook was a shortish, strong, square figure with a pouter-pigeon-like chest that spelt defiance. Powerful legs and thighs, coupled with a deadly throw on the run, made him a brilliant cover point, while his fleetness of foot enabled him both to get into position quickly for the hook stroke and to move down the pitch to slow bowling. Trevor Bailey rated him the third best post-War batsman on a bad wicket after Hutton and Compton. He was a beautiful cutter and scored prolifically from the hook, which however was also often his downfall.

Washbrook stepped into the England side as Hutton's partner in the first Test in 1946, and remained unchallenged until the end of the tour to Australia of 1950–51. The early post-War seasons found him at his most productive. In 1946 he achieved the memorable feat of reaching one thousand runs in the month of July. The following year he hit 2,662 runs, including eleven hundreds, at an average of 68, being nevertheless overshadowed by the record aggregates of Compton and Edrich.

Fortune smiled upon him in 1948, his benefit year. When he went to the wicket in the second innings of the third Test against Australia, at Old Trafford, his place in the team was in jeopardy. Twice he hooked the fast bowling hard and high to Lindsay Hassett on the long-leg boundary, and twice this safest of catchers spilled the chance, relieving the drama the second time by borrowing a policeman's helmet and holding it outstretched. Reprieved, Washbrook scored 85 not out before rain intervened and in all probability saved Australia. Washbrook made 143 and 65 at Headingley in the next Test, and the sportsmen of Lancashire rewarded him with a benefit of £14,000 – which was by far and away a record, and one that stood for more than twenty years.

Hutton and Washbrook opened the England innings in thirty-one Test matches, nearly half of them against Australia's fast bowling attack of those days. Eight times they posted three-figure partnerships, twice doing so in both innings of a match. At Johannesburg in 1948–49 they scored 359 together (in 310 minutes) – which remains an English record. Only one England partnership, that of Hobbs and Sutcliffe, could be said to have exceeded theirs in quality and duration. All six of Washbrook's Test hundreds were begun with Hutton, and when in the 1953 Australian series England went into the field without Washbrook, it was contrary to the wishes of his old partner, now captain.

By 1956 Hutton had retired and Washbrook become a selector, his last Test apparently five years behind him. England's batting, however, was proving fragile against Lindwall and Miller, and his fellow selectors persuaded Washbrook, then forty-one, to turn out once more. Both this comment and his performance were expressive of the man. 'One does not refuse to play for England,' he said, 'but it will not be easy.' The situation was far from easy when on the first morning at Headingley, he joined his captain, Peter May, with the score at 17 for three. By the close, with 201 for four on the board – May 101, Washbrook not out 90 – the clouds had lifted. Next morning he went for 98, but England proceeded to win by an innings, whereupon 'Laker's Match' at Old Trafford ensured that England retained the Ashes. Washbrook's comeback, like that of David Sheppard in the next Test, was a classic example of the wisdom of the chairman of selectors' dictum: when in doubt, go for class.

He had begun his career for Lancashire, aged eighteen, with dangerous brilliancy, scoring 152 against Surrey in only his second county match in the Whitweek of 1933. Not out 135 at close of play, he was called to see the chairman, Tommy Higson, who, after congratulating him, remarked that he would be obliged if he would wear his cap straighter; also, he did not like to see players wearing belts, especially schoolboy coloured ones. Next morning, Washbrook had discarded the belt, but his cap was worn at the same jaunty angle, as it continued to be ever afterwards. The encounter reflects well Washbrook's characteristic blend of conformity and independence.

**Cyril Washbrook: b Barrow, Lancashire,
6 December 1914; d 27 April 1999**

12 OCTOBER 2004
KEITH MILLER
Courage of Our Favourite Aussie
Michael Parkinson

A friend called and said Keith Miller had died peacefully. It was one of the few times he did anything quietly. He was a vigorous and mettlesome man who loved a yarn. Even when illness had shackled him to a wheelchair and reduced his voice to a croak, he never hid from his fellow man. He was a man of great courage, and nothing – not war, or injury, or illness – dissuaded him from his avowed intent to 'only remember the good times'.

He was a perfect hero. As a young man he looked like a god. He was tall and handsome, broad of shoulder, loose of limb; an athlete of grace and style. He hit sixes, caught thunderbolts and bowled like the wind. Most of all he played cricket hard but for fun. Opening the bowling in David Sheppard's first Test match he bowled him a perfect slow googly, first ball. Not quite what the England player was expecting. He once took the field straight from a party wearing black patent leather dancing shoes, and when Don Bradman took guard in his testimonial game expecting one off the mark, Miller nearly took his head off with a bouncer.

When we were both playing for the *Daily Express* cricket team in the late 1950s he would have a tic-tac man standing by the sightscreen so he was kept up to date with the day's racing. He once took an astonishing catch diving across me at second slip, rolling over and handing me the ball. 'I wonder what won that bloody race,' was all he said.

He was, of course, a truly great cricketer, fit to be ranked with the best of the all-time all-rounders. If you marry the ability to the personality, then Keith Miller was incomparably the most attractive cricketer of them all. He was adored particularly in England. If you walked round Lord's with Miller you had better have cancelled all appointments for the rest of the day. Everyone wanted a word, doffed their caps. Keith Miller loved England and the feeling was mutual. He was our favourite Aussie. When Neville Cardus described him as 'The Australian *in excelsis*' he spoke for all of us.

Keith Miller's attitude to life and to the game he played was profoundly influenced by the War. He flew Mosquitos over Germany and survived with a perspective and a set of values that shaped the rest of his life. The way he played cricket in the post-War years was as much a celebration of surviving it as it was the reaction of a man whose lifelong ambition was never to be bored. As he once memorably said: 'When athletes nowadays talk of pressure they only reveal what they don't know of life. They've never had a Messerschmitt up their arse. That's pressure.'

He was not a man for memorabilia. He gave me his last Australian sweater in a plastic supermarket bag. 'Can't think why I kept it,' he said gruffly. His favourite cricket photo – the only one on display at his home – showed the Australian Services team taking the field at Bramall Lane, Sheffield, just after the War. He kept it for when people asked him about the greatest moments in his career. During a subsequent match at Lord's, he would point out from that picture Graham Williams, a tall, skinny man whose first appearance at the venue had come only two weeks after he had been in a prisoner of war camp for four years. As he walked out to bat, the crowd rose to him. Keith Miller said: 'That is my abiding memory. I think of it often. We were the lucky ones.'

I don't want to give the impression Keith Miller was a maudlin man. Nothing would be further from the truth. Of all my friends he had the most extraordinary range of acquaintances. During one pub crawl in Sydney he fell in with a neurosurgeon, a jockey who explained how he won a race by holding on to the arse of the horse in front, a woman of great beauty and title who was obviously smitten by my friend and a war hero who used to fly contraband whiskey concealed in the spare fuel tanks of his plane. He treasured mavericks and was addicted to laughter. Hearing a friend was seriously ill in hospital Keith paid him a visit, smuggling in a bottle of booze. They had such a good time Miller decided to stay the night and was discovered by nurses fast asleep in the patient's bed.

Captaining New South Wales in an up-country game, he attended a civic reception. He addressed the mayor and dignitaries thus: 'I would like to thank the people of ... where the bloody hell are we?' Presenting the prizes at the Greyhound Derby in England he turned up in full morning dress, picked up the victorious animal and kissed it on the nose.

There is a statue to Keith Miller outside the Melbourne Cricket Ground. Don Bradman is alongside. While it would be wrong to portray them as bosom buddies, there is no doubt that – for very different reasons – they are the two commanding figures of Australian cricket. They are both sides of the same coin. Bradman conquering the record books, Miller captivating the populace. Sir Donald loved cricket and business. He believed they were one and the same. Keith loved cricket and Beethoven and would argue the link between sporting and artistic achievement. Keith Miller was a romantic warrior. A proper hero, and a singular man.

**Keith Ross Miller: b Sunshine, Victoria,
28 November 1919; d 11 October 2004**

24 APRIL 1997
DENIS COMPTON
Thank You, Denis – Hero of Cricket
John Major

Fifty years ago in the golden summer of 1947 the Middlesex twins – Compton and Edrich – bestrode English cricket. It was the season Denis Compton scored 3,816 runs for Middlesex at an average of 90.85, and took four centuries off the visiting South Africans into the bargain. And the sun never stopped shining. Until only last month, his third-wicket stand of 370 with Bill Edrich remained the highest partnership against South Africa in Test history.

Denis personified the romance of cricket – a one-off. In the true sense of that overused word, he was a genius. He was a hero to most males now over the age of forty-five, and his dashing batting and good looks had an appeal to the ladies, too. It was said that he and Bill Edrich were as much a match for Keith Miller off the field as on. He was a batsman of flair and instinctive touch who could sweep the most concentrated bowling attack away from any wicket. His balance was perfect and his footwork faultless. Like every great artist, he made it all look so easy.

Denis almost never became a cricketer. It was said that his mother didn't want him to be lounging around the house for the months the game wasn't played, so he signed up for Arsenal. He won an FA Cup medal – on the left wing, alas! – and played eleven internationals for England alongside Sir Stanley Matthews and Tommy Lawton.

He was one of the last, and greatest, of that now vanished breed, the double international. In these professional-obsessed days it is hard to believe, sadly, that they will ever be seen again.

If 1947 was his most prolific run-scoring summer, his crowning year was perhaps when England won back the Ashes in 1953 – Coronation year. Throughout my boyhood he put to the sword – often nearly single-handedly – the best talent from South Africa, Australia and the West Indies.

He made his England debut at the age of nineteen and before the War he became the youngest man to score a century for England. He went on to score 5,807 Test runs, including seventeen centuries, at an average of 50.06. Denis showed unfailing courage in adversity. In 1948 at Old Trafford he edged a ball from Ray Lindwall on to his face and retired bleeding. Later he returned to the crease, his head swathed in crimson, to save the match. 'Compton's knee' became a national preoccupation. Even after his right kneecap had been finally removed, he made 94 in the final Test at the Oval against Australia in 1956.

His last first-class season was in 1957, though his willow still flourished into the 1960s, and he was one of the founding spirits of the International Cavaliers and televised one-day cricket. In the 1950s Denis's debonair good looks made him one of Beecham's first 'Brylcreem boys'. During one match a bouncer from an Aussie fast bowler gave him a few stitches on his forehead. Next morning, standing on an Underground platform, Denis looked up to see a poster of his Brylcreemed hair and smiling face beaming down with one minor addition – an early graffiti artist had inked in a number of stitches.

Denis was never one to mince words. After a recent heavy defeat by Australia he denounced the English team under the headline, 'No pride, no guts, no contest'. But he distanced himself from the 'fuddy-duddies' who just harked back to an earlier era. In 1995 he urged England's selectors to gamble on newcomers: 'This is a game for youngsters. I wouldn't pick anyone over twenty-five.'

Denis was convivial, loyal and a true believer in the game and the values it exemplifies. He lived life to the full. It gave him huge pleasure two years ago to watch his twelve-year-old grandson, Nicholas, on tour in England with his South African prep school. I will miss him greatly as will everyone who knew him. He was an Olympian of cricket. Thank you, Denis. You left memories for all time, even for those who only saw you from afar.

24 APRIL 1997

Life of Colour Played in Dispute with the Clock

Michael Parkinson

It was an official lunch hosted by Denis Compton. We met at 12.30 for cocktails. He wasn't there. One o'clock. Two o'clock. Still no sign. We decided to start without him. Much later, when we were having our cheese and biscuits, he arrived in a bustle. He always seemed to turn up in a cloud of dust even when he was walking with the help of a stick. 'Thank God you started,' he said by way of explanation.

He lived his life in dispute with the ticking clock, whether he was batting in his incomparable prime or counter-attacking the ravages of time and a life lived to the limits. He was not only a great athlete but a natural star. Had he been playing in this day and age there would not have been an unsponsored inch of him, such was his draw.

As a player he was incapable of being on public view without finding something amusing to do. I first saw him nearly fifty years ago at Bramall Lane, Sheffield, where his perceived rivalry with Len Hutton meant he was only grudgingly admired. Len was reckoned to be salt of the earth, Compton something of a glamourpuss advertising hair cream. During a turgid passage of play a dog ran on the field. Compton chased and caught it. As he raised the animal aloft it did what all well-bred Yorkshire terriers do to southern folk: it bit him. As Compton ran from the field for first aid, a wag shouted: 'Put some bloody Brylcreem on it, Denis!'

In recent times we saw a lot of him at our local pub where his old team-mate J.J. Warr holds court. Sometimes he would visit our local cricket club and shake his head with despair at the helmets, body armour and heavy bats. 'Can't pick the bloody thing up, never mind play with it,' he would say. I knew I was getting old when one of our players asked me: 'How good a player was Denis Compton, really?' I said: 'How much time do you have?'

Denis Charles Scott Compton: b Hendon, Middlesex, 23 May 1918; d 23 April 1997

25 APRIL 1986
BILL EDRICH
Man of Courage
E. W. Swanton

William John Edrich, DFC, in all that he did on the field and in war was the personification of determination and courage, the very epitome of 'guts'. His name is coupled immortally, of course, with that of Denis Compton in the Middlesex sides from 1937 until 1958 in one of the most fruitful of all partnerships. Though Compton was as brave a fighter as Edrich when it came to facing Miller and Lindwall, the game came so much more easily to him than to his great friend, and the obvious contrast in method and temperament was part of the fascination to the public of their innumerable partnerships together. Edrich was never a graceful player. He was a good cutter, but with the bottom hand in control his most telling strokes were the hook and the pulled drive. In a tight corner he was apt to overcome technical limitations with an indomitable spirit.

In his first Middlesex season of 1937 Bill scored two thousand runs, as he was to do eight times more, the climax coming with 3,539 in 1947, a total exceeded only by Denis who in that same golden summer piled up 3,816. When in 1938 Edrich scored one thousand runs (all at Lord's) before the end of May an early baptism in Test cricket was certain. It came with disastrous results, his six innings against Australia totalling 67 runs and his first five against South Africa the following winter only 21. Then in the second innings of the last Test at Durban (the 'Timeless' one which lasted ten days) he at last justified the confidence of his captain, Walter Hammond, by making a dogged 219.

As a squadron leader he won the DFC for daylight bombing over Germany, and at the War's end he resumed his cricket as an amateur. Then it was W.J. Edrich who in Australia in 1946–47 established himself as a cricketer of true Test stamp, at number three in the order and also in England's extremity as a fastish bowler propelling that small, tough frame at the enemy as though his lungs would burst. Tests against Australia continued to bring the best out of him, his crowning moment perhaps being the innings of 55 not out which (with Compton at the other end) at last brought the Ashes back home at the Oval in 1953.

His time coincided with an earlier palmy age of Middlesex cricket during which one championship was won, one shared, and second place was achieved four times. In 1951 the partnership of Edrich and Compton jointly took over Middlesex from R.W.V. Robins, under whose brilliant leadership they had been brought up. Captaincy, as also later committee work, was a sphere which came more naturally to Bill than to Denis, and the latter soon dropped out in favour of his friend. Bill Edrich stood for all that was best in cricket: Lord's will not be the same without his cheerful presence.

**William John Edrich: b Lingwood, Norfolk,
26 March 1916; d 24 April 1986**

5 DECEMBER 2011
SAM LOXTON
The Heart of Bradman's 'Invincibles'

Sam Loxton was, even by the standards of his fellow Australians, a fiercely aggressive competitor, both as a hard-hitting batsman and a medium-fast bowler. One of Loxton's finest hours was at Leeds in 1948. England batted first and made 496, with Lindwall, Miller, Johnston and Toshack all returning analyses which are best forgotten. Loxton, by contrast, took three for 55. At one point, having just completed a lengthy bowling spell, he chased a ball to the boundary with such energy that he cannoned into the crowd. Far from being concerned at any damage he might have done to spectators, he caused some amusement by hurling his cap to the ground in disgust at his failure to prevent the four. Such was the spirit which ensured that England, at one time 423 for two, failed to reach 500.

When Australia batted, Bradman went for a mere 33; and with the score at 189 for four, it seemed that England might at last have the all-conquering tourists in trouble. The illusion was brief. Loxton strode to the wicket to join his great friend Neil Harvey, and proceeded to slam 93, an innings which included five sixes. Neville Cardus complained that he got a crick in his neck from watching the ball steepling so high into the stratosphere. Bradman thought that a straight drive off the Lancashire medium-pacer Ken Cranston was the finest six he had seen. When Loxton hit the ball, he observed, in a rather odd comparison, 'it is the music of a sledgehammer, not a dinner gong'. Harvey, still only nineteen, reached his century; and Loxton was so excited that he almost ran himself out in his hurry to leave his crease to shake his young friend's hand. He himself was bowled by Yardley, going for another six – but by that time Australia were on level terms. In the fourth innings, Arthur Morris (182) and Bradman (173 not out) took Australia to 404 for three, and victory by seven wickets.

At the end of the tour, Bradman could hardly praise Loxton enough. 'Did a magnificent job as utility player,' he wrote. 'Very strong physically. Extremely powerful driver and the best player of the lofted drive among the moderns. Tremendous fighter, always throwing every ounce into the game. Fast-medium bowler who could keep going for long spells – on occasions bowled really fast and worried the best batsmen. The most dangerous field in the team. Did stupendous things to get run-outs. I have never seen anyone who had such a powerful throw when off balance.'

As well as that great innings at Leeds, Loxton hit centuries against Essex, Gloucestershire and Middlesex, ending the tour with a batting average of 57.23. Yet he did not find a place in Australia's team until the third Test. The confidence of Bradman's side was well illustrated in the match against Surrey, when the tourists required 122 to win in the final innings. That day, though, the team had been invited to watch the Australian John Bromwich play at Wimbledon. All the players therefore donned their suits to leave the Oval, save Harvey and Loxton, who were sent out to knock off the runs – and Ron Hamence, who padded up in case of a wicket. Harvey and Loxton took less than an hour to win the match, and found the Australian dressing room empty on their return. Loxton relished every moment of the tour, and when the Australians were introduced to the glacially dignified Queen Mary he did not hesitate to ask her to 'watch the dicky bird' while he took a picture. 'You can't say that to Royalty,' a shocked Bradman told him afterwards. 'Well, she cracked a grin for it, didn't she?' Loxton returned.

For twenty-four years from 1955 Loxton was a Liberal-Country member of the state parliament of Victoria. But he never drifted far from cricket, serving as an Australian selector from 1970 to 1981. He then retired to Queensland's Gold Coast, where he umpired and coached in local cricket. In December 2000, Sam Loxton suffered a double tragedy. His beloved wife Joan was found dead in the family swimming pool. Fifteen minutes later, in Fiji, their son Michael died after his left leg was bitten off by a shark.

Samuel John Everett Loxton: b Albert Park, Victoria, 29 March 1921; d 3 December 2011

10 JANUARY 2007
KENNETH CRANSTON
A Brief, Whirlwind Career

Kenneth Cranston decided to give the summers of 1947 and 1948 to playing cricket for Lancashire, performing so well that within three months he was playing for England; within nine he was captaining his country. Cranston had been appointed captain of Lancashire before making his first-class debut. On the field he immediately showed an insouciant flair, both as a hard-hitting middle-order batsman and as a fast-medium bowler. Nor did it harm his reputation that he possessed matinée idol looks.

He instantly became a favourite with the huge crowds who watched Lancashire at Old Trafford in those post-War years. The England selectors, too, were impressed, and after only thirteen first-class matches he was selected for the third Test against South Africa at Manchester. He held his Test place for the rest of series, and at Headingley finished off South Africa's innings with four wickets in six balls. In the winter of 1947–48 Cranston was vice-captain of the M.C.C. team who toured the West Indies. Since the forty-five-year-old captain, Gubby Allen, pulled a muscle on the voyage out, Cranston captained England in the first Test at Bridgetown. *Wisden* awarded him high marks, noting that he set a fine example in the field and that 'little fault could be found with his handling of his limited bowling resources'. England achieved a draw in that match, and Gubby Allen returned to the fray for the second Test, which was also drawn; in the last two Tests, however, the West Indies could no longer be denied. Cranston put in a fine bowling performance in the fourth Test at Georgetown, accounting for Clyde Walcott and Everton Weekes and ending with an analysis of four for 78.

Cranston led Lancashire to third place in the county championship in 1947, and to fifth place the following year. He himself was not far off doing the double in both seasons. But at the end of the 1948 season he remained true to his previously declared intention to leave Old Trafford to join his father's dental practice at Aigburth, in Liverpool. Before that, though, Cranston was perhaps unlucky to be recalled to the England side for the fourth Test at Headingley in 1948, against the all-conquering Australians. The match proved to be a disaster for England (who lost by seven wickets as Australia scored 404 for three in their second innings), and perhaps a step too far for Cranston. To be a glamorous and gifted amateur was one thing; to do battle with Don Bradman quite another. At least, though, Bradman, whose teeth were poor, seemed eager to discuss his dental problems with Cranston.

Kenneth Cranston: b Liverpool, Lancashire, 20 October 1917; d 8 January 2007

17 JUNE 1993
LINDSAY HASSETT
Tough Competitor with
a Dash of Humour

E.W. Swanton

Cricket has always bred characters rich and rare and in any such gallery Lindsay Hassett commands a place all his own. Ray Robinson called him 'Puck in Flannels'. He was five feet six – the height of Hanif Mohammad, and Willy Quaife of earlier days – an inch below his great contemporary Neil Harvey. He showed in his cricket the inner toughness associated with his Australian countrymen, yet could lighten the tensest moments with spontaneous humour. In the 1948 Old Trafford Test the crowd showed their displeasure at some short fast bowling by Lindwall and Miller. Cyril Washbrook hooked high to long leg where Hassett waited underneath just inside the boundary, and dropped the catch. A little later the same stroke was repeated and this normally impeccable fielder dropped it again. Whereupon he removed the helmet from the nearby policeman and held it upside down like an offertory bag: general laughter and the situation defused. In Lahore one very hot afternoon an Australian bowler left the field, returning only hours later when the tail-enders were in. Lindsay fiddled about, moving him, first a little one way, then the other, before finally motioning him back through the pavilion gate.

He batted in two contrasting styles divided by the War. In his early manhood he was a free, uninhibited stroke-maker – not only a brilliant cutter, hooker and glancer, befitting his size. By nimble footwork and precise timing he drove powerfully. He was the only man to hit separate hundreds in a match against the great O'Reilly, going down the pitch and repeatedly hitting over his head.

He made a marvellous start to the England tour in 1938 with successive scores of 43, 146, 148 run out and 220 not out. His first major impact on the Test scene occurred in July at Headingley on a difficult wicket, in atrocious light, with a storm threatening and Bradman and McCabe just out. He went in at 61 for four. Australia needed another 44 to win the match and retain the Ashes, which they did; Hassett contributed a cool 33 in half an hour.

In 1945 he was a sergeant-major when appointed to lead the Australian Services team. He declined a commission, thereby confining himself to Service pay of twelve shillings a day, as against the 16s 6d for Pilot Officer Miller and other officers. Considering that the team – who fulfilled nearly fifty fixtures involving almost continuous travel – brought back a love of cricket to crowds estimated at three-quarters of a million, the wage was a sparse recompense, though it appealed to the captain's whimsical humour.

Hassett was thirty-three when Australian Test cricket restarted in 1946–47. The need for a steadying hand was no doubt a factor in his decision to eliminate all risk from his batting. The touch was still there, the method flawless. Only the aggressive spirit was missing. An inexhaustible patience now brought him all his ten Test hundreds, a number incidentally unapproached after that age by any other Australian. Watching a stubborn innings from the Lord's press box one day, he remarked: 'I'm glad I wasn't up here when I was down there.'

Though he had been an ideal vice-captain to Bradman on the triumphal 1948 tour of England, when it came to the choice of captain for the visit to South Africa in 1949–50 it was said that only the last telegram in a postal vote by the Australian Board of Control ensured his selection. Possibly Hassett's inconsequential manner had ruffled a few dignitaries. At all events this marginal support was made to seem foolish by the overwhelming success of the tour. A fundamental difference of attitude between Australian and South African cricketers in those days was exemplified most starkly in the Durban Test on that tour. South Africa, having made 311, bowled out Australia for 75 but, with a lead of 236, failed to enforce the follow-on. They were then got out a second time for 99. Needing 336 to win, Australia battled away for seven hours and got home by five wickets.

Hassett led Australia in 1950–51 to four victories before F.R. Brown's M.C.C. side broke the monotonous post-War pattern by winning the last Test at Melbourne. The Ashes, after eighteen years, at last changed hands in 1953 at the Oval where England won by eight wickets. Hassett's humorous speech of congratulation to the crowd thronging in front of the pavilion sealed an emotional moment. When, afterwards, an England selector said: 'Well done, Lindsay, that was perfect', he replied with a hint of reproach: 'Yes, not bad considering Tony Lock threw us out.' No Australian team exceeded this one in popularity, nor has any captain left behind warmer feelings of regard and affection.

The only things that broke his composure were breaches of the rigid standards he observed himself and required of his men. In 1981–82 he bowed out of Test commentating, saying that he was fed up with players' misbehaviour. Lindsay's philosophy and that of too many of the moderns were oceans apart.

Arthur Lindsay Hassett: b Geelong, Victoria, 28 August 1913; d 16 June 1993

28 FEBRUARY 1990
LES AMES
The Greatest Wicketkeeper-Batsman
E. W. Swanton

Les Ames was never other than a plain speaker, conspicuously frank and utterly fair. He had no prejudices and was a sound judge of men. His philosophy derived no doubt from a happy boyhood, and from those early formative years in a Kent side rich in character, and with an approach to the game which at this distance seems almost impossibly idealistic. The senior professional over his first twelve summers was Frank Woolley, the most glamorous county cricketer of any generation – what a model for a naturally enterprising young batsman! 'Tich' Freeman, the great leg-spin and googly bowler, was at his peak when Ames began an association with him that was probably the most fruitful in history between wicketkeeper and bowler. Kent, with their professional-amateur mix, were indeed an attractive side, in which Ames's own performance was a main feature.

When he made the first of his six M.C.C. tours, with Chapman to Australia in 1928–29, as the youngest member of the side, it was as understudy to George Duckworth. He owed his first Test caps to his superiority as a batsman. But by the next Australian visit – the Bodyline tour of 1932–33 – Ames was recognised as a master of his craft, equally at home with speed and spin. Of all the wicketkeeper-batsmen, none has bettered his Test average of 40 and eight hundreds. The first of these hundreds, against New Zealand at Lord's in 1931, involved him in a stand of 246 with G.O.B. Allen for the eighth wicket which is still a Test record. Three years later, in an innings of 120 against Australia, also at Lord's, he pulled England out of a hole in company with Maurice Leyland (109).

His achievement of thrice capturing more than a hundred victims, in addition to his habitual thousand runs, must be secure against time. J.T. Murray once got there; no one else. Even more certainly no one will match his sixty-four stumpings in 1932. The next year he made three thousand runs (average 58), but had only sixty-nine victims, handing over at times to another Kent 'keeper, due the following winter to win a Test cap, W.H.V. Levett.

Ames's batting was characterised by nimble footwork and a marked facility of timing, the two being generally complementary, and he loved going down the pitch to the spinners. Against fast bowling he was a compulsive hooker, and thus to some extent vulnerable. He is the only man to have twice won the Lawrence Trophy for the fastest hundred of the season. Both were made in less than seventy minutes. In 1946 a youngster called Godfrey Evans succeeded him behind the stumps. But Ames was batting as well as ever when in 1950, aged forty-four, he scored his hundredth first-class hundred, aptly enough to win a match against the clock in Canterbury Week.

**Leslie Ethelbert George Ames: b Elham, Kent,
3 December 1905; d 27 February 1990**

4 MAY 1999
GODFREY EVANS
An Enduring Talent from
the Age of Innocence

Michael Henderson

One of cricket's mighty oaks was felled with the departure of Godfrey Evans, the Kent and England wicketkeeper. The good fortune of cricketers like Evans was to have played in a more innocent day, when the game was more fun and the players, shielded from the all-seeing eye, savoured life to the full, without fear of intrusion. Evans will be remembered not only as a showman with gloves who played in ninety-one Tests, and belonged to England's strongest post-War team, but also as a man with an irrepressible sense of adventure. Like Denis Compton and Bill Edrich, he believed life was for living.

As a wicketkeeper, he is recognised as the first of the modern greats, standing up to a bowler as quick as Alec Bedser, and flinging himself to both sides, and sometimes in front of the wicket, to hold improbable catches. Bedser and Trevor Bailey, who shared with him some of England's most notable triumphs in the 1950s, considered him the best wicketkeeper they saw, ahead even of Alan Knott. Only five men, Knott being one, have achieved more than his 219 dismissals in Tests, forty-six of them stumped. In all first-class cricket, Evans was responsible for 1,066 dismissals and it was the way he accomplished them, with daring and a hitherto unseen athleticism, that endeared him to a generation of cricket-lovers. He also made 2,439 runs in Tests, with centuries against the West Indies and India.

A handy boxer in his younger days, he first played for Kent in 1939, so he lost five of the best years of his career to the War that began at the end of his first season. After his promotion to the Test side in 1946 he retained his place until the 1958–59 tour of Australia under Peter May, when England lost 4–0. Though he came out of retirement to play briefly in 1967, his career ended properly in 1959. He was not always a dasher. At Adelaide in 1947, as the new boy of the England side, he went ninety-seven minutes without scoring on his way to making 10 not out, which, allied to Compton's hundred at the other end, enabled England's ninth-wicket partnership to save the match. But it was as an enthusiastic striker of the ball that he was best remembered as a batsman. His second Test century, against India at Lord's in 1952, included 98 before lunch. His greatest moment came in Australia on 'Tyson's tour' of 1954–55. After England had lost the first Test in Brisbane by an innings and 154 runs, a match Evans missed with sunstroke, he assured his team-mates on the plane: 'Not to worry. We shall be there at the finish.' True to his word, he struck the boundary at Adelaide that retained the Ashes.

Len Hutton, the captain of that outstanding side, recalled later the qualities that made Evans such a good team man. 'He'd be keeping wicket all day in Sydney, 95 in the shade, and never miss a thing. Like the rest he would stagger off the field, have a bath, get dressed, have a drink, sit down at the piano in the hotel and start to play. He was ready for the evening. That is what you need on tour.' Hutton's observation is worth bearing in mind these days when England tourists have been known to sit in their rooms all afternoon, or mooch no further than the pool. On the recent trip to Sharjah, a member of the England one-day party declined an invitation to go on a desert safari by saying: 'I'd rather lie down in the bunker of a golf course.' They were made of sterner stuff in those post-War days, which is why players of a certain vintage find it hard to understand why their successors seem so po-faced. If you have fought a war, as those men had, playing cricket was a bonus and their gratitude was reflected in the cavalier manner of their play.

It was not all jolly good fun; it never is. England – and Evans – earned success against Australia the hard way. In 1948, the wicketkeeper missed stumping Morris, then Bradman, as Australia scored 404 to win the fourth Test at Headingley. Eventually, they regained the Ashes at the Oval in 1953, when Evans was a fully established member of a side who, from this distance, look as proud a team as England have had. Led by Hutton, they were buttressed by Compton, Edrich and the young May, with Bedser, Trueman, Laker and Lock to bowl. In the middle, providing balance, was Evans. He was not the first wicketkeeper Kent supplied to England, nor the last. Les Ames played forty-seven Tests behind the stumps but, as he was a good enough batsman to make 102 hundreds, there were other reasons for his selection. Evans's only real rival as England's most distinguished gloveman is Knott, whose ninety-five Tests brought him 269 dismissals. For anybody who grew up watching 'Knotty', it is hard to imagine that any wicketkeeper could have performed better, or for a longer period of time. Nevertheless, E.W. Swanton, selecting his 'team of the century' for *The Cricketer* magazine's seventieth anniversary in 1991, preferred Evans to his successor.

In later years, the bewhiskered Evans set the odds at Test matches for Ladbrokes, which in 1981 led to the bookmakers making the celebrated offer of 500–1 against England to beat Australia at Headingley. Two members of the Australian team took them up before Ian Botham and Bob Willis pulled off one of cricket's most remarkable victories. To the very end, Evans was seen around cricket grounds, home and away. To English spectators in Australia this winter he was a familiar figure, at the match and in the hotel bar, happy to recall the days when England were not always second best. He will be recalled with gratitude by those who admired him as a lissom youth. He played his part. He must be numbered in the song.

**Thomas Godfrey Evans: b Finchley, Middlesex,
18 August 1920; d 3 May 1999**

4 JANUARY 2011
KEITH ANDREW
The Supreme Technician Behind
the Stumps

Keith Andrew played for Northamptonshire between 1953 and 1966, and was regarded by many good judges as the best wicketkeeper in the country. Yet he played in only two Tests. Partly this was because Godfrey Evans was unassailable during the 1950s as first choice for England behind the stumps. Evans, flamboyant and inspirational, was always at his best on the big occasion. Hurling himself in all directions, he specialised in seemingly impossible catches. Andrew, by contrast, was the supreme technician who made everything look easy. He never squatted down, but stood with his hands near his knees, ready to seize any chance with elegance, speed and economy. His concentration rarely failed.

To some extent this very competence counted against him. Frank Tyson, his friend and colleague in the Northamptonshire team, admitted he preferred bowling with Evans behind the stumps. 'He does drop more, but the way he makes catches puts me right on top of the world as a bowler. Keith is so methodical and easy, you hardly realise you've taken a wicket.' On the county circuit, however, Andrew was widely regarded as the more reliable 'keeper. Doug Wright, the formidable leg-spinner who played with Evans at Kent, said that, day in, day out, he would have preferred to bowl with Andrew behind the stumps: 'His performance was always top class.' On the other hand, 'put Godfrey in a Test match, and he was the best of the lot'.

Andrew, a clever but supremely modest man, was wholly incapable of advertising either himself or his claims. Nor was he, either in character or background, the kind of cricketer liable to attract strong support from such arbiters of the game as E.W. Swanton. His reward, however, was to become one of the most admired and respected cricketers among his professional peers.

Indeed, when in July 1954 Andrew was chosen for the coming tour of Australia and New Zealand, he had played only twenty-six first-class matches. On the way out to Australia, Len Hutton took the trouble to tell him that he was strictly second-choice wicketkeeper. Having delivered this judgment, the captain hardly spoke to him for the rest of the tour. As it transpired, Godfrey Evans fell ill just before the first Test, at Brisbane, and Andrew made his debut for England. In Alec Bedser's third over he missed an extremely difficult chance given by Arthur Morris, who went on to make 153 out of Australia's 601 for eight. After England had lost by an innings and 154 runs, the finger of blame was most unfairly pointed at Andrew. He played in only four more games during the remaining three months in Australia. The disdain of *Wisden* was sadly undisguised: 'Andrews [sic] lacked Evans's effervescence, but he was neat and efficient in an ordinary way.'

From 1955 to 1963 various 'keepers were preferred to Andrew by the England selectors: Arthur McIntyre, Dick Spooner, Roy Swetman, Jim Parks, John Murray, Geoffrey Millman and Alan Smith. Yet all that time Andrew's reputation grew among connoisseurs. In 1962, against Lancashire, he became only the second wicketkeeper to take seven catches in a county championship innings. Moreover, in 1965 when he captained Northamptonshire to second place,

Andrew, despite often standing up on uncovered wickets, went seven matches without conceding a bye. At last, after forty-odd hours in the field, some 900 overs and 2,132 runs, a delivery flew over his shoulder in the eighth match.

Keith Vincent Andrew: b Oldham, Greater Manchester, 15 December 1929; d 27 December 2010

31 DECEMBER 2009
ARTHUR McINTYRE
Career Overshadowed by
Godfrey Evans

Arthur McIntyre's wicketkeeping played a crucial part in Surrey's seven successive championship triumphs from 1952 to 1958. He was unfortunate that the panache and brilliance behind the stumps of Godfrey Evans, who was two years younger, prevented him playing more than three times for England. Many good judges, however, felt that there was little to choose between the two wicketkeepers. Peter May, in his autobiography *A Game Enjoyed* (1985), seemed to go further than that: 'Godfrey Evans could touch great heights of wicketkeeping, but day in, day out, Arthur was the most reliable wicketkeeper of the 1950s. He should have played many times for England. He kept superbly to Alec Bedser, Loader, Laker and Lock on difficult wickets, and made it look easy. He was never acrobatic. There was no need, as he was always in the correct position on his two feet.' Alec Bedser echoed these sentiments, considering McIntyre 'at least equal to Evans' in his ability to make stumpings off his brisk medium pace. McIntyre, in fact, found it more difficult to keep wicket to Jim Laker, who spun the ball so viciously. In a first-class career that embraced 390 matches between 1938 and 1963, McIntyre claimed 638 catches (nearly all of them as wicketkeeper) and 157 stumpings.

On leaving school he at first took a job outside cricket because he did not fancy selling scorecards or pushing the roller as a member of the Oval ground staff. When he did finally go to the Oval, in 1936, he was put in charge of the cycle shed. It was as a bowler that McIntyre made his debut for Surrey in July 1938, at home against Sussex; he claimed the wicket of the Sussex number eleven. In his next game, against Kent, the opposition included Frank Woolley, then fifty-one years old. His lingering bowling ambitions were rather dampened by the Bedser twins (also serving in Italy at the end of the War) who bluntly observed that his height – five feet five – was something of a handicap. Nevertheless, he became firm friends with the Bedsers, between whom, incidentally, he found no difficulty in distinguishing: Eric, he noticed, had a slight scar under his chin.

On the twins' recommendation McIntyre wrote to Surrey asking if, on his return, he might be considered as a wicketkeeper. After Gerald Mobey's retirement at the end of 1946 season, McIntyre immediately established himself as the county's wicketkeeper. His batting steadily improved, and in each of the three seasons from 1948 to 1950, he made more than one thousand runs. In 1950 McIntyre and his wife Dorothy dined with Godfrey Evans, and Dorothy jested that it was high time Godfrey suffered an injury which would give Arthur a chance to play for England. Shortly afterwards Evans broke his thumb, and McIntyre was selected to play in the fourth Test against the West Indies at the Oval. 'You witch,' Evans told Mrs McIntyre. England were comprehensively defeated at the Oval. Yet, while McIntyre failed with the bat, he kept wicket so well to Doug Wright's fast leg-breaks that he was chosen as Evans's deputy for the tour of Australia in 1950–51. On the way out, he hit a brilliant century in fierce tropical heat against Ceylon at Colombo. It was still extraordinary, though, that he should have been preferred to Gilbert

Parkhouse for the last batting place – Godfrey Evans kept wicket – in the first Test in Brisbane. With England caught on a sticky wicket, McIntyre was out for only one. In the second innings he joined Len Hutton, who was batting brilliantly, as England sought a winning total of 193. Sickeningly, though, McIntyre was run out going for a fourth run, as the Australian wicketkeeper, Don Tallon, ran fifteen yards to collect a bad throw, and then threw down the wicket with his gloved hand. England lost by 70 runs, with Hutton left not out on 62.

McIntyre continued to play regularly for Surrey until 1958 (when he was one of *Wisden*'s Five Cricketers of the Year) and occasionally thereafter. His last first-class match was against Yorkshire at Bramall Lane, Sheffield, in July 1963: he made 50 not out (in a Surrey total of 225) against an attack that included three England bowlers, Don Wilson, Ray Illingworth and Brian Close. Geoff Boycott, in his second season for Yorkshire, also featured in that game, though he contributed nought and two. Boycott would retire from first-class cricket in 1986; that was eighty years after the debut of Frank Woolley, with whom McIntyre had also played.

Arthur John William McIntyre: b Kennington, London, 14 May 1918; d 26 December 2009

17 MAY 2001
GIL LANGLEY
Unorthodox, but the Safest
of Wicketkeepers

The Australian Gil Langley was one of the safest wicketkeepers to don gloves. Stocky, like so many of his trade, the balding Langley did not otherwise resemble an international sportsman. His girth was more than ample; his shirt tails invariably disengaged themselves from his trousers. One commentator, seeing him at Lord's, wondered whether an apple farmer had strolled into the hallowed precincts. Nor was Langley's style of wicketkeeping orthodox. He would squat down with his right foot flat and his left heel raised. His gloves did not rest on the ground in the usual manner, but were held in front of his knees. It did not seem that such a burly, chaotic figure could possibly react quickly enough to snap up a difficult catch.

Godfrey Evans, his opposite number in the England team, thought Langley 'one of the most untidy-looking 'keepers I have ever seen'. Yet there was no questioning Langley's efficiency, or the favour he found with bowlers. What he lacked in mobility, he made up in anticipation; what he lacked in panache, he made up in security. If he never had Evans's genius for bringing off seemingly impossible catches, there was no surer bet in the bread-and-butter business of wicketkeeping.

Though Langley played in only twenty-six Tests, he claimed

ninety-eight dismissals (eighty-three caught, fifteen stumped). His average of 3.77 dismissals per Test is unrivalled. Langley's finest performance was in the Lord's Test of 1956, when he participated in nine dismissals (eight caught and one stumped). This remained a Test record for nearly quarter of a century. Langley's feats were accomplished in a solid, no-nonsense manner. He was no showman; even his appeals were muted. But there was nothing muted about his character. Big-hearted and cheerful – an almost Dickensian figure – he was always popular with other players. He would later turn this likeability to account as a politician.

Gilbert Roche Andrews Langley: b Adelaide, South Australia, 14 September 1919; d 14 May 2001

25 JUNE 2011
JOHN WAITE
South Africa's Greatest
Wicketkeeper-Batsman

John Waite was the most outstanding wicketkeeper-batsman in South Africa's Test history. Tall, thin and seemingly frail, Waite appeared an unlikely wicketkeeper – until he went into action. Unobtrusively efficient when standing up to slow bowlers (though the great off-spinner Hugh Tayfield posed plenty of problems for him as well as for batsmen), he was capable when standing back of spectacular catches off South Africa's fast men, Neil Adcock and Peter Heine. Waite played in fifty Tests between 1951 and 1965, the first South African to reach that mark. For a long time his total of 141 victims (124 caught, seventeen stumped) in Tests was unequalled by a fellow countryman, though it was eventually overtaken by David Richardson and Mark Boucher. He shares, with Boucher, the South African record of twenty-six victims in a Test series, a total he achieved against New Zealand in 1961–62. As a batsman, Waite possessed all the strokes, notwithstanding a limited backlift, being particularly strong off his legs. In Tests, however, he was frequently obliged to demonstrate the soundness of his defence.

Cricket in South Africa was not for the sensitive. Invited in December 1949 to turn out for a South African XI against the touring Australians in Durban, Waite took time off from Rhodes University to appear in the match. Arriving in the dressing room, he put down his bag, only to see it thrown out of the window by the great batsman Eric Rowan, whose niche he had unwittingly usurped. 'This is my place,' Rowan shouted, 'and don't you forget it.' Later in the match Rowan was vastly amused by the swelling on Waite's shoulder after he had been hit by a bumper from Keith Miller.

Waite was chosen as reserve wicketkeeper for South Africa's tour of England in 1951. But in his first match, against Yorkshire, he established his claim to the Test side when, opening the batting, he made 31 out of the South African total of 76. No other batsman showed anything like his skill against the bowling of Bob Appleyard and Johnny Wardle. In the first Test at Trent Bridge, Waite scored a creditable 76 before being run out. There were no congratulations in the dressing room. 'You could have got a hundred,' his captain, Dudley Nourse, told him. 'You want to keep your bloody mind on the job.' In fact, the umpire, Frank Chester, had made an error in giving Waite out.

Shortly afterwards, against Lancashire, Waite and Eric Rowan batted with painful slowness in an opening stand of 164. When the spectators began slow handclapping, the batsmen sat down on the ground. Subsequently Rowan dilated in no uncertain terms on the manners of the Old Trafford crowd. The South African management reacted by threatening him with banishment from the rest of the tour. He was saved, however, by the support of the younger players – with Waite to the fore. The commentator Charles Fortune speculated that it was due to this incident that Waite was never offered a leading role – not even as vice-captain – in the South African Test side.

John Henry Bickford Waite: b Johannesburg, 19 January 1930; d 22 June 2011

10 FEBRUARY 2011
TREVOR BAILEY
One of the Great All-Rounders

Trevor Bailey was England's leading all-rounder after the Second World War and known as Barnacle Bailey because of his dedication to the forward defensive stroke; he subsequently made a living from the game as an author, journalist and (for more than thirty years) commentator on *Test Match Special*. In the popular estimation Bailey's reputation for leaden batting tended to obscure his rare talent as a bowler – fast-medium with a model high, sideways-on action which encouraged outswing. At his best he could touch greatness, and never more so than in the first innings of the fifth Test at Kingston, Jamaica, in 1954. On a docile pitch he took seven for 34, shooting out the powerful West Indies batting – Garry Sobers came in at number nine – for 139, and enabling England to square the series.

First with Alec Bedser, and then with Fred Trueman, Brian Statham and Frank Tyson, Bailey was one of a quartet of fast or fastish bowlers who established England as the leading force in Test cricket from 1953, when the Ashes were regained after a gap of twenty years, to 1958–59, when the Australians unexpectedly snatched them back again. Bailey's batting was by no means uniformly dour. 'He would be quite content to play sound, steady cricket,' observed *Wisden* in 1950, 'but circumstances have tended to make him into an aggressive player.' Circumstances most certainly changed in the seasons that followed.

At the crease Bailey had the capacity to manufacture a crisis where none existed, and to prolong it beyond reason or advantage. Against Australia at Brisbane in 1958, he batted 357 minutes to reach 50 – still the slowest half-century in first-class cricket – before being dismissed for 68 in 458 minutes. On the other hand, there were occasions when Bailey's concentration and determination proved invaluable, most memorably in the Lord's Test of 1953 when his fifth-wicket stand of 163 in four and a quarter hours with Willie Watson on the last day saved England from defeat. When Bailey, on 71, was finally caught essaying a cover drive, his annoyance was plain for all to see. Bailey's defensive batting again proved crucial in the fourth Test of the same series, at Headingley. In the last innings he prevented Australia from winning against the clock by bowling six overs down the leg side off a long run. He was always the toughest and most combative of cricketers. Moreover, his excellence as a fielder matched his efforts as a bowler and batsman. Several times he took stunning catches which helped to turn a Test.

He played for the XI at Dulwich in his first year at the school. It was a strong team who won all their school matches; that fanatical old boy P.G. Wodehouse treated them to dinner in the West End, followed by a show at the London Palladium. In 1939 Wodehouse watched Dulwich play St Paul's, the last game of cricket he saw (save in a German camp), and, as he reported in *The Alleynian*, 'probably the dreariest ever seen on the school grounds'. The horror was still with him twenty-two years later, when he told Alistair Cooke that 'T. Bailey played a dreadful innings'.

After serving in the Royal Marines during the War, and subsequently coming down from Cambridge, Bailey was employed by Essex as assistant secretary, and from 1964 to 1969 he would be secretary of Essex. On the field he was particularly successful in 1949, achieving the 'double' of one thousand runs and one hundred wickets, the first of eight times that he would perform this feat, and winning an England cap in the four Tests against New Zealand. In his first Test, at Headingley, he took six for 118 in New Zealand's first innings, while at Lord's he hit a fine 93, outshining even his partner Denis Compton. In August, playing for Essex at Clacton, he took all ten Lancashire wickets.

But the ultimate test for all English cricketers comes against the Australians. Bailey first encountered the old enemy in 1948, playing for Cambridge University, and showed his mettle with a fighting 66 not out. Since he was appearing for Essex against the tourists in the next match, he travelled from Cambridge to Southend in the Australian team coach – an experience, he later wrote, which involved a considerable degree of culture shock. On the first day at Southend the Australians scored 721, with Bradman helping himself to 187. Bailey was at first disappointed by The Don's apparent lack of stroke play, until he looked at the scoreboard and discovered that he had reached fifty in no time. For the rest of his life Bailey insisted that Bradman should be placed in a category far above any other batsman.

Some critics felt that Bailey's bowling would be punished in Australia. In the series of 1950–51, however, he performed superbly in the first two Tests, taking thirteen wickets for only 137 runs. It was a harsh blow for England when his thumb was fractured by a ball from Ray Lindwall in the third Test. Having played a key part in regaining the Ashes in 1953, Bailey helped England retain them in 1954–55 and 1956. He enjoyed another successful series in South Africa in 1956–57, when he opened the batting against the ferocious attack of Neil Adcock and Peter Heine. At Lord's the next summer, on a lively pitch, he destroyed the West Indies' batting with match figures of 11 for 98. He again opened the innings in four Tests in Australia in 1958–59, but experienced a poor series and was never chosen for England again.

That Bailey was far from finished became abundantly clear in 1959, when he scored more than two thousand runs and took more than one hundred wickets, the last time this feat has been achieved. He played on for Essex until 1967, when he was forty-three. Statistically, the best all-round performance of his career was in the match against Hampshire at Romford in 1957. Essex made 130 (Bailey 59) and 141 (Bailey 71 not out) against Hampshire's 109 (Bailey six for 32) and 116 (Bailey eight for 49). Still more impressive, perhaps, were his figures against Yorkshire at Headingley in 1960, when he top-scored in both innings (60 not out and 46) and returned seven for 40 and five for 61, to help Essex defeat the champion county by 57 runs.

When Bailey retired in 1967 he had made 28,641 runs (including twenty-eight centuries) and taken 2,082 wickets. In the entire history of cricket only nine men (including William Astill, W.G. Grace, George Hirst, Wilfred Rhodes, Maurice Tate and Frank Woolley) have achieved twenty thousand runs and two thousand wickets; and only three (Bailey, Fred Titmus and Ray Illingworth) have achieved the feat since the Second World War. In addition, Bailey held 425 catches. He was also one of a select band to have passed both one thousand runs and one hundred wickets for England.

Trevor Edward Bailey: b Westcliff-on-Sea, Essex, 3 December 1923; d 10 February 2011

5 APRIL 2010

ALEC BEDSER
A Gentle Giant Whose Timeless Values Still Inspire

Derek Pringle

Few bowlers get to be knights of the realm and, as Sir Alec Bedser used to point out, not always in jest, he was the first since Sir Francis Drake. The honour was thoroughly deserved, not just for his selfless deeds as a bowler for Surrey and England but for the lifelong loyalty to a game he cherished deeply. In a sporting era where materialistic rewards were few, his playing career was the very epitome of service, a foreign word to most modern players. His 236 Test wickets were the most taken by the time he played the last of his fifty-one Tests in 1955. His total would have been even greater but for the Second World War denying him the opportunity to take advantage of his physical prime.

A big man, fifteen stone and six foot three, his bowling was based on rhythm and economy, being brisk rather than quick. Inswingers and a nagging accuracy were his main weapons, though their effectiveness increased once he learnt to bowl the leg-cutter by wrapping his enormous fingers around the seam. It was a leg-cutter that famously dismissed that other cricketing knight, Sir Don Bradman, for a duck at Adelaide in 1947. Bradman, who remained a lifelong friend, maintained it was the best ball that ever got him out. Mostly Bedser's rewards were borne of hard toil, his first-class tally of 15,539 overs – the many he bowled in Australia comprising eight balls – making today's workloads pale by comparison. In an era where fast-bowling support was sparse he ascended to greatness without a regular partner. Often over-bowled, as he shouldered the roles of strike and stock bowler, he became the willing shire horse who occasionally won the Derby.

Bedser was twenty-seven when he made his Test debut against India at Lord's in 1946 after playing just seven county championship matches. He presented himself at the Grace Gates having lugged his bag from the station and then, just as matter-of-factly, announced himself by taking twenty-two wickets in his first two Tests. Just as now, the Ashes were the main prize and his crowning achievement was to see them won back in 1953 after nineteen years in Australia's possession. His thirty-nine wickets in that series, Coronation year, was an Ashes record until Jim Laker, his Surrey team-mate, bettered it three years later.

With no central contracts, and with loyalty to county as great as to country, Bedser regularly bowled more than one thousand overs in a season – one of the reasons Surrey won the championship eight times during his career. 'Bowling as often as possible is how you become a proper bowler,' he used to say. The mores of modern cricketers, with their gym work and protein shakes, never ceased to amaze him and his identical twin, Eric, who pre-deceased him by four years. The shock of the new rarely failed to draw comment from the pair in their eyrie at the Oval, though their critique was nearly always pertinent. One favourite gripe was about the stream of England fielders who require a lavatory break during Tests due, apparently, to modern theories of rehydration. 'I once bowled thirty overs in Adelaide in 100-degree heat and afterwards I drank thirty tins of Fosters and never had a pee,' he would say. Another favourite from Adelaide used to crop up whenever players were whingeing about the heat. 'You think that's hot. We once played at Adelaide where you couldn't get the ball out of Godfrey Evans's gloves because the rubber had melted.'

For younger generations he could come across like one of the old codgers in the *Muppet Show*, moaning away uproariously in the wings, but only because he had such high principles. His life, and that of fellow cricketer Eric, was based on dedication and discipline, which is why they disliked fuss, frippery and the decline in standards both believed endemic in modern life. His devotion to his brother, Surrey, and England, was legendary. As well as a playing career that spanned twenty-one years between 1939 and 1960, he gave twenty-three years' service as an England selector, twelve of them as chairman.

Fittingly, Bedser's legacy still has resonance today in the form of a letter he wrote to Geoff Miller, the current national selector, after dropping him from the England side. 'It is a prized possession,' Miller says. 'Apart from outlining the reasons why I'd been dropped it also encouraged me to keep performing in county cricket and to not lose heart. It was so considerate I use it as a template now whenever I need to let players know they've been left out.' Another Miller story concerns the time he drove Alec, then manager of England's 1979–80 tour of Australia, to Sydney airport to pick up Eric. 'I'd heard all the stories about how they always dressed identically and no one but their mum could tell them apart,' said Miller. 'We got there and Eric was wearing the exact same suit, shirt, tie, shoes and socks. Whether there'd been a phone call between them before the plane left London, I don't know, but I spent the rest of the trip unwilling to commit to using their first names for fear of getting them wrong.'

With Bedser's passing, English cricket has lost an icon. It is perhaps the fate of subsequent generations of cricketers to misinterpret those who have gone before but Alec was always honourable and well-intentioned in everything he did – values almost as rare in the modern game as his famous leg-cutter.

Alec Victor Bedser: b Reading, Berkshire, 4 July 1918; d 4 April 2010

16 MARCH 2011
PETER LOADER
The Bowler 'Who Could Make
a New Ball Talk'

Peter Loader opened the Surrey bowling with Alec Bedser and played a leading part in the county's seven successive championship victories between 1952 and 1958. A fiery character, 'Scrubs' Loader never pretended to like batsmen. Tall and wiry in build, and with a long high-stepping run, he generated relentless hostility, alike in word and deed. Yet he was also a highly skilful bowler, capable of producing late movement in flight. 'Loader could make a new ball talk,' Jim Laker remembered. 'He had the uncanny knack of bowling an outswinger from both close to the stumps and also from the very end of the return crease, and he was able to do the same thing with the inswinger. No quick bowler of his era could better his change of pace, and he could often bowl successively a slow off-spinner and the most vicious of bouncers.' Occasionally there were doubts (which Jim Laker shared) about the legality of Loader's action when delivering bouncers. Moreover, he was liable to lose his temper, and with it his control.

Greatly feared on the county circuit, Loader did sterling service for Surrey. He was unlucky to play at the same time as Brian Statham, Frank Tyson and Fred Trueman. As a result he was chosen for only thirteen Test matches, beginning with the fourth Test against

Pakistan in 1954. That winter he did well in Australia and New Zealand, taking forty-one wickets at 19.92 apiece without gaining a place in the Test attack, dominated by Tyson and Statham. Loader did not conceal his irritation at Len Hutton's decision to treat him as a second-string bowler. But in 1955, when Tyson was injured, Loader was picked for the fourth Test against South Africa, and took four for 52 in the first innings. And when Surrey played Yorkshire at the Oval that summer, he sent Len Hutton back to the pavilion for scores of nought and one.

The high spot of his career came in the fourth Test against the West Indies at Leeds in 1957, when he bowled Frank Worrell and Everton Weekes in the same over, claimed Garry Sobers as his next victim, and then finished off the innings with a hat-trick, clean bowling J.D. Goddard and Roy Gilchrist, and having Sonny Ramadhin caught by Trueman. This was the first hat-trick by an England bowler in a home Test match since J.T. Hearne performed the feat against Australia at Headingley in 1899. And not until 1995 did Dominic Cork follow suit, against the West Indies at Old Trafford.

In the winters his county captain Stuart Surridge, whose family firm made bats, used to commandeer Loader for tree-felling. The idea was to build his strength. 'After the first three days,' Loader told Hampshire's Malcolm Heath, who had also been invited, 'you'll want to run away and die. Your hands will be sore and bleeding, and your back will ache more than you can imagine. But it does get better.'

Peter James Loader: b Wallington, Surrey, 25 October 1929; d 15 March 2011

25 MAY 2006
ERIC BEDSER
The Overshadowed Twin
was No Slouch

Eric Bedser was older by ten minutes than his identical twin brother Alec; and it was perhaps only chance which decreed that, while Alec became the mainstay of England's bowling in the years after the Second World War, Eric did not progress beyond county level. As teenagers, both Bedsers bowled medium-fast. Deciding, however, that some variation was required in the fraternal armoury, they tossed a coin to decide which twin should continue to bowl in this style, and which should take up another mode of attack. The spin of the coin favoured Alec, so Eric thenceforward concentrated on bowling off-breaks. A better batsman than Alec, he won a place in the Surrey side as an extremely useful all-rounder.

Had Eric Bedser been playing for any other county, he would surely have done the 'double' (one thousand runs and one hundred wickets) several times. But with Jim Laker and Tony Lock as team-mates, opportunities for another spinner were limited. Only when these two great bowlers were away playing for England did Eric Bedser have much of a chance with the ball; and his performances on these occasions played a crucial role in Surrey's seven successive county championship titles. Indeed in 1956 (Laker's *annus mirabilis*, when he claimed nineteen wickets in a Test match against Australia), Eric Bedser actually had the better bowling average for Surrey, taking sixty-eight wickets at 17.22 apiece, against Laker's fifty-seven at 18.17. No wonder that Stuart Surridge, Surrey's captain, observed that without Eric Bedser Surrey might not have carried off the title.

Undoubtedly, Eric Bedser could have found a better career for himself away from Surrey, save that neither twin would contemplate separation for any length of time. As though anxious to emphasise that they were both sprung from the same egg, they invariably wore the same clothes, and enjoyed the frequent confusion of their identities. Though they sometimes exchanged sharp remarks on the field – 'Rubbish, bowl straighter, Alec, make them play,' Eric would shout from slip – and were unsparing in criticism of each other's golf shots, the bond between them was indissoluble. Eric delighted in Alec's greater success as though it had been his own: 'Our absolute and complete affinity is hard to explain,' he once wrote, 'but is true and very real to us. Our lives have been so close that we are, for all purposes, one. We share everything and have never quarrelled seriously.'

In 1950 Eric was selected to play for The Rest against England in a Test trial at Bradford. That was the game in which Jim Laker took eight wickets for two runs in the Rest's first innings of 27. One of those two runs came from a full toss which Laker served up to allow his county colleague to get off the mark. It was said that Alec Bedser ran several yards back at mid-on to facilitate the single. In the second innings Eric top-scored with 30. He would never play for England, but when he accompanied Alec on M.C.C.'s tour of Australia in 1950–51 he found himself called up due to injuries to play for M.C.C. against Tasmania. There was no story-book ending, however; he made only two and took no wickets.

As the 1950s wore on, and Alec's bowling lost some of its zip, there were seasons (1956, 1957, 1959 and 1960) when Eric finished above his twin in the Surrey bowling averages. In 1961, after Alec had retired, Eric took seventy-two wickets, more than in any other season.

**Eric Arthur Bedser: b Reading, Berkshire,
4 July 1918; d 24 May 2006**

15 APRIL 1992
STUART SURRIDGE
A Confident, Combative Captain

E.W. Swanton

Alec Bedser has recorded how before W.S. Surridge started his first season as captain, he made this entry in his diary: 'Surrey will be champions for the next five years.' To me the story -- egotistical as it is – rings true. For of all Surridge's virtues as a leader a bounding self-confidence was paramount. What is more, the prophecy came true: Surrey won the county championship in all five seasons of Stuart Surridge's captaincy, and in the following two summers when Peter May took over.

Surridge certainly had at his disposal two great bowlers in Alec Bedser and Jim Laker, and another, soon to make his name for England, in Tony Lock. Peter Loader, another Test bowler, came a little later. Surridge also had a batsman of top pedigree (but only one) in May, and a wicketkeeper, Arthur McIntyre, scarcely inferior to Godfrey Evans. In the Surrey side he inherited were a few reputedly awkward personalities. They did not remain so for long.

In the post-War euphoria, big crowds flocked regularly to the Oval to see the attacking cricket on which Surridge insisted. His instinct was aggressive in all respects, especially in the fielding. The strong bowling was supported by four brilliant close catchers – Lock, Ken Barrington, Mickey Stewart and, not least, the captain himself. John Warr, his opponent in many a tough fight, has described Stuart Surridge as 'an enthusiastic extrovert buccaneering risk-taker'. I would add only that, in truth, the keenness on the field at tense moments sometimes grew rather too fierce – slightly akin to what one deplores today.

Surridge inherited and greatly expanded the family bat-making and sporting equipment firm. Many a schoolboy first took guard with a bat bearing the legend 'Stuart Surridge'. On his Suffolk property he grew willow trees.

Walter Stuart Surridge: b Herne Hill, South London, 3 September 1917; d 13 April 1992

31 MARCH 1995
TONY LOCK
Spinner's Tale that Batsmen Misread

Christopher Martin-Jenkins

Tony Lock was a member of the most famous of all England's spin-bowling combinations. Lock and Jim Laker were every bit as important a reason for England's success in the 1950s as the fast-bowling combinations with whom they performed. Both were also devastatingly successful members of the Surrey side who won the county championship in each season between 1952 and 1958. In 1955 alone Lock took 216 wickets at 14.39.

Lock in his prime was reddish-haired and fiery, an orthodox slow left-arm bowler with a rapid faster ball and a fast bowler's spirit. His appeals would rent the skies above the Oval and his flexible frame would bend back in anguish, one hand thrown across his eyes, if a batsman narrowly escaped him with a fortuitous edge. He spun the ball sharply, especially, if by no means exclusively, on the sometimes dusty Oval pitches of his era. But his consummate skill was proved later when he rejuvenated Leicestershire with his vibrant personality and shrewd captaincy in the mid-1960s and when he did the same for Western Australia, for whom he played from 1962 to 1971.

The latter achievement was perhaps his most remarkable, because the word had got round that Lock threw his quicker ball – a legacy, it is thought, of winter practice in nets with a low roof – and he remodelled his action to get wickets by flight and guile where once they had come from potency of spin. When he retired after seventy-four matches for Western Australia, he had taken more wickets for them than anyone.

Lock's wonderful agile close fielding, notably at short-leg, was his other special glory, though his orthodox right-handed batting was often useful to Surrey and England, not least against the West Indian fast bowlers in England in 1963 and again in the Caribbean in 1967–68 when he was called from Australia to play in the last two of his forty-nine Tests.

He took all ten Kent wickets at Blackheath in 1956, the year in which Laker twice performed the same amazing feat against the Australians. Only eight bowlers, two of them also left-arm spinners, have taken more wickets in a career than his 2,844. Lock would have played in even more Tests but for another left-arm spinner in Johnny Wardle of Yorkshire, a generally better bowler on hard wickets overseas, though not, perhaps, than the bowler Lock himself became on those sorts of surfaces in the second phase of his colourful career.

Graham Anthony Richard Lock: b Limpsfield, Surrey, 5 July 1929; d 30 March 1995

28 DECEMBER 1994
PETER MAY
The Purest of Amateurs Who Showed Professionals the Way

E.W. Swanton

P.B.H. May acts as a poignant reminder of better days. Three times in the 1950s he took part in successful Ashes series, twice under Sir Leonard Hutton and once when he had succeeded him as England's captain. Before Peter May's retirement, aged thirty-two, the Ashes pendulum had swung back. Yet his tally of twenty Test victories (ten defeats and eleven draws) tops the list among England captains.

The strength of Peter's leadership was his own example. He was not only the best player technically, the pick of that fine post-War flowering of amateur batsmen, but in temperament a perfect example of watchful unremitting concentration. As a captain he reflected the qualities of his predecessor, orthodox, conventional if at times over-inclined to defence, tough behind an unfailingly courteous exterior.

Like most who rise to the top of the tree, Peter was a prodigy from earliest schooldays at Charterhouse where he had the luck to come into close contact and friendship with the old England and Leicestershire cricketer, George Geary. Thence may be derived his understanding of and affection for the professionals who played under him for Surrey and England, chief among them his comrade-in-arms and Surrey vice-captain Alec Bedser. The purest of amateurs himself, he never forgot that their livelihood depended very much on his consideration and his personal performance. He was the antithesis of the legendary carefree amateurs.

National Service in the Navy preceded Cambridge where he made an immediate mark as a footballer as well as a cricketer. He was twenty-one when in his second year at the university he opened his Test career with the first of his thirteen hundreds and 4,537 runs in sixty-six matches for England.

**Peter Barker Howard May: b Reading, Berkshire,
31 December 1929; d 27 December 1994**

16 APRIL 2005
CHARLES PALMER
Rapier-Like Batsman with a Sideline in Donkey Drops

Charles Palmer might have looked (in Trevor Bailey's words) 'a natural for the role of hen-pecked bank clerk in a farce'; in fact, he was a fine batsman for Worcestershire and Leicestershire, a peculiarly effective occasional bowler, and a highly competent administrator, elected president of M.C.C. in 1978–79. Only five feet seven inches tall, slightly built, bespectacled and with a soft, almost apologetic voice, Palmer possessed deceptively strong wrists which could send the ball racing to the boundary with the cut. Equally, he could dispatch overpitched deliveries with sweetly timed drives.

Two fine innings for the Gentlemen against the Players at Lord's underlined his rare talent. In 1952 he scored 127, showing himself perfectly at ease against an attack including both Alec Bedser and Derek Shackleton, two superb exponents of medium-fast bowling, as well as the equally renowned spinners Jim Laker and Johnny Wardle. In 1955 Palmer did even better, wielding his bat like a rapier as he plundered the Players' attack for a brilliant 154.

He played only once for England, in the second Test against the West Indies at Bridgetown, Barbados, in 1954. England were heavily defeated, with Palmer following his 22 in the first innings with a duck in the second. Though England managed to square the series, it was a notoriously unhappy tour. In part the trouble stemmed from the dour approach of Len Hutton, the England captain. But Palmer, who had been sent to the West Indies as player-manager, also drew opprobrium for failing to discipline the rowdier elements in the side, and to put a stop to the foul-mouthed sledging.

At the end of April 1948 he had played the most significant innings of his life for Worcestershire, threatening to make a century before lunch against Don Bradman's Australians, whose attack included Ray Lindwall, Keith Miller and Ernie Toshack; in the event he fell for 85. At the end of the tour Bradman commended this 'splendid exhibition of strokeplay'. Though Palmer did little else in 1948, the England selectors, eager at that period to promote amateur talent, chose him for the tour of South Africa in 1948–49. Palmer took time to find his form in South Africa and failed to make the Test side.

His slow-medium bowling was always accurate and occasionally deadly. Against Surrey, the county champions, at Leicester in 1955, he put himself on for an over in spite of a bad back, to allow two other bowlers to change ends. Surrey were then 42 for one. Making use of a damp patch just outside the off stump, Palmer immediately claimed the wicket of Peter May, and decided to persist. In no time he had taken eight wickets for no runs, all but one clean bowled. Of Surrey's last pair of batsmen, Jim Laker had claimed the best first-class analysis for a bowler taking eight wickets, conceding only two runs when playing for England against The Rest at Bradford in 1950. Laker now took a violent swing at Palmer and was dropped in the covers, thus depriving the bowler of an analysis of nine for nought. After that, Laker edged some runs, so that Palmer's final analysis read fourteen overs, twelve maidens, seven runs and eight wickets. Palmer then made 64 out of 165 in Leicestershire's second innings, and, when Surrey batted again, bowled thirteen overs for one run. Even so, Leicestershire lost by seven wickets.

Palmer was an expert in the art of donkey drops, which he would send towering up twenty feet or so in the air, aiming to land the ball on the top of the batsman's wicket. He took several wickets with this unlikely form of attack, notably for Leicestershire against the West Indies in 1957, when his donkey drops accounted for Rohan Kanhai, Frank Worrell and Nyron Asgarali.

Charles Henry Palmer: b Old Hill, Staffordshire, 15 May 1919; d 31 March 2005

21 APRIL 2001
BERT SUTCLIFFE
New Zealand's Very Own Don Bradman

Bert Sutcliffe was the golden boy of New Zealand cricket, a batsman of dazzling gifts; the course of his career, however, shows what a cruel game Test cricket can be. Fair-haired and good-looking, the tall and slim Sutcliffe was a left-hander who possessed all the strokes – best of all a classic off-drive – and an absolute determination to use them. He reached his peak on the New Zealanders' tour of England in 1949. Patsy Hendren, watching him massacre the bowling in the nets at Lord's before the season began, prophesied he would score two and a half thousand runs that summer. In the event, Hendren proved 127 runs short of the mark.

On the slow pitches of May, Sutcliffe showed a tendency to get out to the hook shot, but as the weather improved (1949 was an exceptionally dry summer) he achieved a remarkable consistency for so dashing a player. The moment of transformation came on 17 June, when the New Zealanders had to make 109 runs in thirty-five minutes to beat Hampshire. They reached this total with four minutes to spare, thanks to an astonishing innings from Sutcliffe, who hit three sixes and four fours as he raced to 46 in thirteen minutes. The next day he scored 187 against a Surrey attack who included Alec Bedser and Jim Laker.

Six further centuries followed that summer, including one in the third Test at Manchester. By August Sutcliffe was in such form that he reeled off successive scores of 243 and 100 not out against Essex; 88 and 54 in the fourth Test at the Oval; 61 and 79 not out against Lancashire; 40 and 12 not out against Kent; and 59 and 110 not out against Middlesex, the joint county champions. In the four Tests, all of which were drawn, Sutcliffe was equally consistent, scoring 423 runs from seven innings for an average of 60.42. His average for all first-class matches for the tour was 59.70; at the time only Don Bradman had scored more runs on a tour of England. Moreover, Sutcliffe's fielding, whether close to the bat or in the deep, was invariably brilliant.

The series of 1953–54 in South Africa proved to be the turning point in Sutcliffe's career. On Christmas Eve 1953, New Zealand suffered its worst rail disaster when 151 people were killed, among them the fiancée of Bob Blair, one of the team's bowlers. The side were still coming to terms with the tragedy on Boxing Day when, at Johannesburg in the second Test, they were caught on a flying wicket by the pace of Neil Adcock and Peter Heine. Up to that moment Sutcliffe had always played fast bowling with skill and courage, but at Johannesburg he had only made nine when he was struck behind the left ear by a ball from Adcock and taken to hospital. Twice he fainted; nevertheless he returned to the crease with his head bandaged, and hit seven sixes and four fours in a remarkable 80 not out, scored out of 106 in 112 minutes. There was, however, a hint of desperation about the performance, and in those days without helmets he never regained confidence against the fiercest pace bowling. Sutcliffe went on playing Test cricket until 1965, and on easy batting wickets against bowlers of moderate pace could still dominate. But the dream of the golden boy who could put any attack to the sword had gone forever.

Bert Sutcliffe: b Ponsonby, Auckland, 17 November 1923; d 20 April 2001

27 AUGUST 2006
CLYDE WALCOTT
The West Indies' Great Ambassador
Scyld Berry

Sir Clyde Walcott, one of the 'three Ws' who empowered West Indian cricket, was the most powerful batsman of his time. In the era before heavy bats became commonplace, Walcott stood out as the most intimidating batsman of his generation. Immensely strong, Walcott stood up and flayed bowling off the back foot, while Everton Weekes pulled and whipped it, and the third member of the triumvirate, Sir Frank Worrell, cut and caressed it. Three great batsmen from one small island in the Caribbean Sea: this was a marvel in itself. For the trio to appear and play at the same time was a miracle, and in the process they raised the West Indies from the rank of also-rans into a power who defeated England and ran Australia close.

The first sign of the feast to come was in 1945–46, when Worrell and Weekes put on 574 for Barbados against Trinidad, a record stand for any West Indian wicket in first-class cricket. All three Ws made their Test debuts in the 1948 home series against England. By the time he had finished in 1960, Walcott had scored 3,798 runs at an average of 56 in his forty-four Tests, with fifteen centuries.

In his early days he was also a wicketkeeper, agile for all his size, and he was able to read the spin of Sonny Ramadhin, as few England batsmen could do. He prefaced today's era in that he was a 'keeper who could bat, averaging 40 in Tests when he wore the gloves. When he did not, Walcott averaged 66, as high as anybody after Sir Donald Bradman. Such was his versatility that sometimes Walcott took off the wicketkeeping gloves and bowled. He took eleven Test wickets at 37 each, besides fifty-seven catches and eleven stumpings. And to complete the all-round package he became manager of the West Indies World Cup-winning teams of 1975 and 1979, an I.C.C. match referee and the first non-English president of the International Cricket Council.

But it will be as a batsman above all that Walcott will be remembered, his physique mirrored in the glassy, grassless pitches which used to grace the Caribbean islands. His apogee was the 1954–55 series against Australia in the West Indies when he hit five centuries – the first batsman to hit five in a Test series – with an aggregate of 827 runs in the five Tests. Australia had Ray Lindwall and Keith Miller to bowl, too, and to drink with the West Indians after play in those glad, calypso days.

**Clyde Leopold Walcott: b Bridgetown, Barbados,
17 January 1926; d 26 August 2006**

13 MAY 2004
ALF VALENTINE
The Master of the Art of Spin Bowling
Colin Croft

If you were born male in the West Indies in the mid-1950s, as I was, one had no choice but to be inundated with the names of the 'three Ws': Everton Weekes, Frank Worrell and Clyde Walcott. Also ingrained in the memory for eternity were the names of two spinners – the Trinidadian Sonny Ramadhin, who supposedly bowled right-arm off-breaks but was also known to put in the regular leg-break and who usually bowled with a cap on and sleeves rolled down; and the seemingly always smiling, bespectacled Jamaican, the original 'Toothpick', Alfred Valentine, who bowled orthodox left-arm. The pair, Ram and Val as they became known, were the bowling tormentors after the three Ws had bludgeoned and caressed runs galore when the West Indies toured England in 1950 and won a Test in the United Kingdom for the first time.

Now Val is no longer with us. Personally, I have lost a friend, while the West Indies have lost one of their greatest names and cricketing figures, one who actually created West Indies cricketing history, even folklore. Of the approximately two hundred and seventy (only) West Indian Test cricketers since the team's inception in 1928, Valentine and Ramadhin will always have their names twinned for their exploits in 1950. So revered were the two spinners – Valentine was twenty then and Ramadhin twenty-one – that they were celebrated firstly by Lord Beginner, a Trinidadian calypsonian living in the UK, with: 'Those little pals of mine/Ramadhin and Valentine.' The better-known Lord Kitchener also sung a great ditty after the West Indies had won the second Test of the four-Test series at Lord's, thus levelling the series. 'Ramadhin, you deserve a title; Ramadhin, followed by a medal; And we can't leave behind; the invincible Jamaican, Valentine.'

Few who saw the photographs or the newsreel films of the celebrating West Indians as they crossed the hallowed turf of Lord's on that summer's day on 29 June would forget the crowds, with their guitars and noisemakers. What a celebration that was. The statistics of Ramadhin and Valentine on that tour were astounding when compared to modern-day cricket. The West Indies won the series 3–1 and in that historical Lord's Test, Ramadhin had match figures of 115–70–152–11. Valentine's returns for that game were equally mind boggling – 117–75–127–7. In the four Tests, Ramadhin bowled 377.5 overs and Valentine an incredible 422.3 overs, capturing, respectively, twenty-six wickets at 21 apiece and thirty-three wickets at 20 apiece – totally surreal stuff. They bowled about two hundred overs between them in each Test! These guys must have been bowling with Exocet missiles since the ball hardly left the playing square. It was of little wonder that Valentine was selected as a *Wisden* Cricketer of the Year in 1951.

Alfred Valentine only played in thirty-six Tests from 1950 to 1962 and took 139 wickets at an average of 30.32 from approximately 2,158 overs. His economy rate (runs scored per over) though, is stupendous – 1.95. He could place the ball on a coin delivery after delivery. Oh, for such accuracy now in West Indies cricket. In 1996, when Jamaican Pat Rousseau came to be president of the West Indies Cricket Board, he effected an unprecedented event. He invited all of the living West Indies Test cricketers to a banquet in

Jamaica. Of course Val was there, the life of the huge party, a single embodiment of being West Indian and then a West Indian cricketer. Afterwards, in 1998, I actually played a few benefit games with the then seemingly indestructible Valentine – who had retired to Miami – in Lauderhill, Florida, and again he held court. I know I will miss him, but his legend as a West Indian cricketer and history-making icon will live forever.

Alfred Louis Valentine: b Kingston, Jamaica, 28 April 1930; d 11 May 2004

20 JUNE 2002
SUBHASH GUPTE
The Spinner Garry Sobers Thought
the Best He Faced

Subhash Gupte was considered by no less an authority than Sir Garry Sobers to be the finest wrist spinner he batted against. This assessment is all the more striking when it is remembered that Sobers fought many a duel against Richie Benaud. Moreover, in his autobiography Sobers goes even further, judging Gupte to have been a better bowler than Shane Warne. Gupte, however, played in only thirty-six Tests for India, and rarely enjoyed the luxury of belonging to a dominant batting side who left him plenty of runs to bowl against. He performed against formidable opponents on perfect batting wickets, under captains who sometimes failed to set sensible fields and with fielders who were often unreliable. Even so, after only eighteen Tests he had ten times taken five or more wickets in an innings – a feat he achieved only twice more in the latter part of his career. It took him only twenty-two Tests to reach the mark of one hundred Test wickets. Such was his early dominance that Mihir Bose, in his *History of Indian Cricket*, refers to the period 1953 to 1956 as 'The Age of Gupte'.

Hero-worship spawned imitation, and Bishan Bedi was only one of the great Indian spinners of the next generation to find inspiration in their predecessor's career. Gupte seemed a small and slight figure to bear the weight of so much renown. Yet his frail, spidery physique lent itself to a classical high-armed action, the only oddity in which was a curious skip as he released the ball. He relished long spells, and never suffered from sore fingers, being very much a wrist rather than a finger spinner, with the ability to turn the ball on even the best batting wickets. His bowling combined unvarying accuracy of line and length with every permutation of flight and spin. Shane Warne, Sobers points out, is far flatter through the air than Gupte; in addition Gupte mastered not only leg-break and top-spin, but also two different types of googly, one bowled with a lower arm. As he would also bowl the occasional leg-break with a lower arm, batsmen were none the wiser.

After a period out of the Test team, Gupte was recalled at the end of 1961, and against England at Kanpur showed he had lost none of his skill as he took five for 90, including a spell of four for six in eighteen balls. He was still only thirty-two, and still seemed to have a long international career in front of him. But in the next Test at Delhi he got into trouble after a hotel receptionist complained of being harassed over the telephone by one of the Indian players. The call in question was traced to the room which he shared with Amritsar Kripal Singh. Gupte, in fact, was wholly innocent. Riled, though, by the suggestion that he should have prevented Kripal Singh from bothering the receptionist, he reacted by giving a member of the Indian Board of Control the rough side of his tongue. He was informed that he would not be selected for the forthcoming tour of the West Indies. He never represented India again.

**Subhashchandra Pandharinath Gupte: b Bombay,
11 December 1929; d 31 May 2002**

24 MARCH 2004
DENNIS BROOKES
Northants Batsman Who Amassed
Nearly 31,000 Runs

Dennis Brookes was a fine batsman and a stalwart of Northamptonshire cricket – as a player from 1934 to 1959 (captain 1954–57), as coach and captain of the Second XI in the 1960s, and as president of the club from 1982 to 1984. Upright in stance, unruffled in demeanour, 'Brookie' adopted the same calm, dignified approach at the crease as he showed in life. When, after the War, he opened the batting for Northamptonshire, he managed, in the words of his Essex counterpart Dickie Dodds, 'to make the fielding side feel that to bowl a bouncer to him was an affront against decency'.

Brookes scorned brute force, gathering runs almost imperceptibly with elegant drives and subtle deflections. As a young man, it was said, he had hooked and pulled, but in maturity such extravagances were excised. From his 925 first-class innings, Brookes amassed 30,874 runs – a number exceeded by only fifty-six players in the history of the game – at an average of 36.10. His seventy-one centuries included one against every county. His record was the more remarkable in that he was playing for a county who for the first nine years of his career (1934–39; 1946–48) finished bottom of the table seven times, and second bottom twice. Indeed from May 1935 to May 1939 Northamptonshire did not win a single match. Brookes well remembered the game against Leicestershire, at Whitsun 1939, when the long run of failure in the championship was broken. He had a boil on the neck, but, as he recalled, 'in those days if you didn't play you didn't get paid'. His stoicism was rewarded when he made 187, and his side swept to their first victory against another county for four years. 'Northants break a bad spell', recorded the local *Chronicle and Echo*, with some understatement.

Yet despite Northamptonshire's dreadful record, Brookes stood out as one of the best batsmen in the country. Chosen for M.C.C.'s tour of the West Indies in 1947–48, he scored a century in his second game, but was unlucky enough to chip a finger in the first Test. When the doctor caused an infection by strapping the injured finger to another, Brookes's tour – and, as it transpired, his Test career – was over.

Despite Northamptonshire's continuous run of defeats, Brookes remembered the carefree nature of pre-War cricket with great affection. At the Oval, for example, Surrey laid on as many drinks at lunch as the players wanted. 'They used to have Pimms No. 1,' he recalled, 'and some of our senior players used to be a bit high by the time they went out in the afternoon. They stopped that later on.'

When the county championship resumed in 1946, Brookes scored 115 in his first innings, against Middlesex at Lord's. Promoted to open the batting, he became the first batsman to score more than two thousand runs for Northamptonshire in a season. Many deemed him unlucky not to be chosen for M.C.C.'s tour of Australia in 1946–47. By the time Brookes retired from first-class cricket in 1959, he had scored 28,980 runs for Northamptonshire, more than anyone else in the county's history. He exceeded one thousand runs in a season seventeen times, and two thousand runs six times. His best season was 1952, when he compiled 2,229 runs at an average of 47.42.

As captain of Northamptonshire's second XI, Brookes was able to bring on such players as Peter Willey and Wayne Larkins. With his innate modesty, 'Mr Brookes' was greatly esteemed and much liked by all who encountered him. It seemed entirely appropriate that he should sit on the Bench in Northampton. His judgments on cricket reflected his experience in the game. 'English cricket was at its best in the 1950s,' he reckoned, looking back on nearly seventy years at Northampton. 'Things that have destroyed the game are the covering of wickets, the introduction of one-day cricket (which spoilt the skills of it) and of course the grassroots (no cricket played in state schools). Cricket is a lifetime's job. You can't suddenly become a good cricketer at twenty-three or twenty-four.' For years Dennis Brookes and his wife Freda lived in a house the back gate of which opened on to the members' car park at the Northampton ground.

**Dennis Brookes: b Leeds, Yorkshire,
29 October 1915; d 9 March 2006**

3 JUNE 2012
FRANK PARR
Promising Cricketer Lost to
the Jazzman's Lifestyle

Frank Parr played cricket for Lancashire in the early 1950s and was good enough to be considered for the England Test team; but his growing involvement in the jazz scene, eventually as trombonist with the Mick Mulligan Band, put paid to his chances of a professional career. In *Owning Up* (1978), the second of his volumes of autobiography, George Melly, the band's frontman, explained why Parr's time as a star wicketkeeper was short-lived. The professional cricketer, Melly observed, 'is expected to behave within certain defined limits. He can be a "rough diamond", even "a bit of a character", but he must know his place. If he smells of sweat, it must be fresh sweat. He must dress neatly and acceptably. His drinking must be under control. He must know when to say "sir".' Frank Parr, Melly observed, had none of these attributes: 'He was an extreme social risk, a complicated rebel whose world swarmed with demons and Jack O'Lanterns', and he 'concealed a formidable and well-read intelligence behind a stylised oafishness'. His fellow band members, Melly recalled, never knew the reason for Parr's quarrel with the captain of Lancashire which ended his cricketing career, 'but after a month or two in his company we realised it must have been inevitable'.

Parr kept wicket in the Lancashire first team from 1951 to 1954, achieving ninety dismissals for the county. A left-handed batsman, his highest score was 42, against Sussex at Hove. Parr impressed the England selectors, and after a strong performance at the Oval in 1952 was tipped to play for the Test side. In 1953 he came close to being selected for the winter tour of the West Indies. The former England wicketkeeper Herbert Strudwick described him as 'the most promising 'keeper I've seen in years'. But Parr combined his cricket with a jazzman's lifestyle, Lancashire's fast bowler Brian Statham recalling him as 'an arty, untidy type who looked what he was, a spare-time musician'.

Parr's scruffy attire and laid-back manner were tolerated by Lancashire's easy-going captain Nigel Howard, but when Cyril Washbrook took over in 1954 he demanded higher standards of dress and behaviour. Parr was dropped after just five matches, and Washbrook even warned Worcestershire (who offered Parr a job, but then withdrew the invitation) against taking him on: 'I should inform you,' Washbrook wrote, 'that he can be a grave social risk.' Yet as a cricketer Parr was at the height of his powers. 'I thought it was the end of the world,' he recalled. 'It's probably why I took up serious drinking.'

Parr played with the Merseysippi Jazz Band for six years before joining the Mick Mulligan Band in 1956 as a full-time professional and moving to London. In the 1950s George Melly and the Mulligan band became synonymous with a jazz lifestyle that involved imbibing copious amounts of alcohol and frenetic and varied sexual activity at all hours of the day and night. Inevitably the band's performances were often affected, and the attendant disasters were sometimes spectacular (on one occasion, when playing solo trumpet, Mulligan was so drunk that all he could do was blow hard and very loudly, producing thirty-two bars of ear-shattering cacophony); yet as

CDs of the period show, by the late 1950s Parr had become a gifted performer.

By then, however, the band's brand of revivalist 'trad' jazz was going out of fashion. '[We] knew something was up when we did a concert with Tommy Steele,' George Melly recalled later. 'We did our set and the audience was quieter than usual. Then Tommy Steele came on and these small girls exploded into shrieks. Our trombonist, Frank Parr – famously depressive – said we would all be on the breadline.' The band shut up shop in 1961, and Parr soon gave up playing for good. For ten years he was Acker Bilk's manager, then worked selling advertising space before having walk-on parts on television shows such as *Psychoville* (2009), and in films, including *The King's Speech* (2010).

**Francis David Parr: b Wallasey, Cheshire,
1 June 1928; d 8 May 2012**

20 SEPTEMBER 2001
T.C. 'DICKIE' DODDS
The Lord's Great Entertainer

T.C. 'Dickie' Dodds was a dashing opening batsman for Essex between 1946 and 1959; what made him unique, however, was that he hit sixes in accordance with his religious convictions. 'Personally,' observed Archbishop William Temple, 'I have always looked on cricket as organised loafing.' And certainly most cricketers determined to dedicate their lives to God have turned away from the flannelled fools at the wicket. 'My heart was no longer in the game,' explained the England Test player Charlie Studd after his conversion in the 1880s. 'I wanted to win souls for the Lord.' And though the Reverend David Sheppard allowed himself to be lured back to Test cricket by the prospect of a tour to Australia in 1962–63, that was only a temporary dereliction of duty. But when Dodds joined Moral Re-Armament in 1946, he took the view that the best way to glorify God was to bring the right spirit to cricket (albeit not on Sundays).

The game, he explained, 'should be a creative activity: it is meant to be a reflection of the Greatest Creator. The more a player reflects the nature of the Creator, the more creative he becomes. My battle as I played cricket was always to try to bring myself under God's control, to make not my will, but God's, operative.' Such was the philosophy that caused Dodds to become one of the post-War game's greatest entertainers, described by Colin Welch as a *'beau sabreur*' and 'the Cyrano de Bergerac of the eastern suburbs'. He was a man who, while frankly admitting his fear of the bumper, was invariably inclined to deposit it in the crowd. Against Dodds, even a great bowler like Brian Statham could find his first two deliveries dispatched for four and six. 'Hey, Dick, what's going on?' demanded that least malignant of fast bowlers. Conversely, Dodds was not a bit surprised that selfish batsmen, who thought only of their averages, drove away the crowds. Was not crude materialism always self-defeating in the long run? Listening to the wireless one day, he was delighted to hear Ian Botham describe how he achieved his great feats against Australia in 1981. 'You've got to enjoy it, let it speak for itself, let it take you over,' Botham said. 'You know, Dickie,' a priest told Dodds later, 'that is a perfect expression of the Holy Ghost.'

His father, a keen cricketer capable of bowling right-arm medium or left-arm slow at will, was vicar at Riseley; his grandfather had been organist at Queen's College, Oxford. Dodds grew up in a large vicarage where the gardener could be co-opted as bowler, and the boy was soon a cricket enthusiast. In the summer of 1939 he turned out for Middlesex Second XI. In those days he was chiefly a leg-break bowler; all cricketing ambitions, however, had to be shelved with the outbreak of the Second World War. Dodds served with the Signals in India and Burma. His skill with ciphers gained him a commission, and he ended the War as a captain. In Bombay he played for a Service XI, captained by Douglas Jardine, who had led England on the Bodyline tour of Australia in 1932–33. When Dodds's leg-breaks were hit all over the ground, he asked Jardine if he could move a fielder on the boundary. Jardine was furious: 'You and I are amateurs,' he barked. 'It is only professionals who ask to have their field shifted when they are hit for four.'

Dodds took part in the advance on Mandalay, and helped to execute the signals deception prior to the capture of the enemy base at Meiktila. He also became involved with a girl who, as he wrote in his autobiography, 'had frequently been in the glossy social magazines of India'. It was perhaps his unease about this affair that helped to turn his mind to religion. His girlfriend could not approve of this development, and when he returned to England she presented him with a book of risqué stories in the hope, as she put it, that he was still capable of enjoying such things. Later she married a general.

In England, Dodds was introduced to T.N. Pearce, the captain of Essex, who invited him to a trial at Chelmsford. In the spring of 1946, sitting in his father's garden at Hatton, Dodds underwent the religious experience which changed his life: 'I decided that, so far as I could understand it, I would from that point only do what God told me to do.' Demobbed on 20 May 1946, Dodds turned up two days later for his first match, against Sussex at Ilford. That night, after being out for 18 in the first innings, he seemed to receive a clear instruction in his prayers: 'Hit the ball hard and enjoy it.' For some weeks, though, he continued to play cautiously, even while conscious that 'a God who loved beautiful things could not love the dull old cricket which I played'. The turning point came when he and Sonny Avery put on 270 for the first wicket against Surrey, with Dodds hitting his maiden century and winning his county cap. A few matches later, batting against Middlesex, he said: 'I felt closer to God than ever before in my life. I tried to fashion the loveliest stroke I could manage for the God who would enjoy them. In return I had a tremendous sense of His pleasure.'

Dodds played as an amateur in 1946, but turned professional at the end of that season. He spent his winters working with Moral Re-Armament, first in London, then in the industrial areas of Britain, and later in India, Australia, America and Europe. His benefit in 1957 realised £2,325, which he immediately turned over to

Moral Re-Armament. Much of it was spent in India. Though Dodds went prematurely grey, his attitude to cricket remained perennially youthful, and he contributed largely to Essex, twice winning the *News Chronicle* Award for Brighter Cricket.

Thomas Carter Dodds: b Bedford, 29 May 1919; d 17 September 2001

6 DECEMBER 2000
COLIN COWDREY
A Gentle Man from a Gentler Age
Michael Henderson

Michael Colin Cowdrey grew up batting at the St Lawrence Ground in Canterbury in the 1950s, so he knew all about the Elysian Fields as a young man. Now that he has passed away, he can join the ghosts of other run-stealers as they flicker to and fro. For those of a certain age, Cowdrey's cover drive, recollected through the haze of an August afternoon, was more than a thing of beauty. It was, and it remains, a stroke to unlock the memory; a memory, intangible yet always present, of the game as it was and as it can be, like some promise of endless summer.

That Cowdrey belonged to a gentler age is a given, and he was its Don Quixote: courtly, chivalrous, modest. Of the English batsmen who grew to maturity in that much misunderstood decade, Peter May was the most gifted, Tom Graveney the most elegant, Ken Barrington the most stubborn and Cowdrey the most puzzling. He shared May's gifts and Graveney's elegance but there was a diffidence in his manner that he could never quite overcome. Team-mates told him, and opponents knew, that he never understood how good he really was. Figures give some indication of his talent.

He was the first cricketer to play one hundred Tests and he marked that hundreth appearance by scoring a hundred against Australia. No Englishman has made more than his twenty-two Test hundreds, or held more catches (120). Only three England players have exceeded his aggregate of 114 caps. He made more tours to Australia, six, than any other player, English or otherwise, and he took six of his Test hundreds off the West Indies. He led England twenty-seven times between 1960 and 1969 and, in all first-class cricket, he made 42,719 runs in a career that began in 1950, when he was seventeen and ended twenty-six years later.

Cowdrey's first Australian visit, in 1954–55, was disrupted by the death of his father, who had pointedly given him those famous initials: M.C.C. Leonard Hutton, as he then was, took the young man under his wing and the first of Cowdrey's Test centuries came on that tour, at Melbourne. His last trip, twenty years later, was an ordeal that no batsman of forty-one should have to endure. On hard, bouncy pitches he went in first against Dennis Lillee and Jeff Thomson, who bowled faster on that tour than anybody has done, before or since. Cowdrey's response was to introduce himself in the middle to Thomson thus: 'How do you do? My name's Cowdrey.'

Yes, he belonged to a gentler age but it would be wrong to suggest that Cowdrey was an innocent. There was nothing half-baked about the bowlers he faced and, on the famous occasion in 1963 at Lord's, when he went out to face a rampant Wes Hall with his broken arm in plaster, he demonstrated considerable courage. Even in his twilight years, in 1975, he was a fine enough batsman to make a century at Canterbury against the touring Australians. A year later he played his last game for Kent, the county he captained for fifteen consecutive seasons, and upon his retirement he published a best-selling autobiography. At the time there was no figure more closely identified with English cricket. He remained active in the last two decades of his life. M.C.C. conferred the presidency of the club upon him and, as chairman of the International Cricket Council, he presented himself as a conciliator in a rapidly changing cricketing world. Indeed, as Graeme Wright, the editor of *Wisden*, wrote of Cowdrey's travels: 'He has spent more time on the road than the Grateful Dead.'

When Cowdrey began his career the professional apartheid of gentlemen and players was still in existence, and a club such as Yorkshire could sack a bowler as fine as Johnny Wardle for comments he made in a book and then prevent him from playing for any other county. Those were not always the good old days. But when cricket-lovers summon up an image of Cowdrey in full sail, and they will, in their thousands, they may recall a kinder, gentler, less hysterical game, peopled by players who laughed more than they scowled. For many the passing of this much-loved man will carry them back down 'the happy highways where I went, and cannot come again'.

9 DECEMBER 2000

Modest Man of Integrity Who Nurtured Spirit of Game

David Sheppard

Colin Cowdrey was a dear friend and the news of his death came as a great personal blow, as I know it did to his many friends. He was a man who stood for all that is best in cricket, as a great player and then, after he had stopped playing, as an administrator. He never spared himself in working for the good of the game at every level. Last year he introduced a debate in the House of Lords on the development of excellence in sport in Britain. Colin didn't often sound passionate, but on this occasion he spoke with rare passion about widening opportunities for young people.

When I was seventeen, I went to Lord's Cricket Ground and watched one of the schools matches that used to happen there. It was Clifton against Tonbridge and this tubby boy of thirteen was bowling leg-spinners and googlies for Tonbridge. He took eight wickets in the match and scored 75 and 44 against the eighteen-year-olds. He bowled quite beautifully – with a skill that he never quite recovered later on. All the cricket world knew about this prodigy – and often doubted whether such precocious talent would bring any lasting achievements. In the event Colin lasted longer in Test cricket than anyone of our generation. We were on opposite sides at Oxford and Cambridge and for Kent and Sussex, and we batted together in a number of matches for England. My mother and Colin's mother watched cricket together, finding warmth on cold days from a rug that Colin's mother had knitted.

The final comeback of my unusual cricket career was the 1962–63 tour of Australia, with Ted Dexter as captain. Colin and I were very close by this time. We took time each week to talk and share our faith, pray and read the Bible together. There were many ups and downs for me as a player on that tour but one of the ups was in the Melbourne Test, which we won. Colin and I had a partnership when we ran a lot of short singles together. He wasn't athletic, though he was a natural ball-games player. He was quite a solid figure who would not have won any races, but he was the best runner between wickets I batted with. I made up my mind that if he called me for a run I would always go, and would never consider sending him back. He was the only player whose judgment I reckoned I could trust enough to do that – and we never got into trouble.

Three years ago, after I had retired from Liverpool, Colin said to my wife, Grace, that he wanted to give us a tree to celebrate our retirement and to remember our Melbourne partnership. Now at the bottom of our garden there is a red acer, 'Crimson King', which is a lovely reminder to us of Colin and his friendship. On the Sunday of that Test match, I preached at a sportsmen's service in Melbourne Cathedral: Brian Booth, of Australia, read one lesson and Colin read the other. During the match three centuries were scored – made by the three of us who had taken part in the service. Afterwards Bobby Simpson said to me: 'I'm beginning to think that after all there must be something in this that I didn't know about.'

Colin Cowdrey was a fine catcher close to the wicket. He took great pleasure in making no fuss about it. He would catch the ball and almost look the other way as though nothing had happened. He was, too, a careful student of the game. Len Hutton was his captain when he was a very young member of the England side in 1954 and he learnt a great deal from the way Len batted and thought about the game. I think there were times when, as a batsman, Colin became introspective; given the skill he possessed, there were occasions when he might have dominated bowlers, rather than allow them to crowd the fielders round him. That was perhaps part of his over-modest character. He was never a domineering person.

He showed me the form of service used at his mother's funeral, not many years ago; at the end there was a quotation of something she had said to her grandchildren and the last words were 'and work hard'. I realised that was how Colin had been brought up, with a massive work ethic and tremendous sense of duty. I understand that his ambition in his last few days was to 'make it' to a dinner that was raising charitable funds for the hospital where he had been treated. He made it to the dinner just two or three days before he died. That was characteristic in that he found it very difficult to say no if he was asked to do something. He had a powerful sense of obligation.

He would keep me posted about the game. We had many

discussions about England's struggles or successes. As a bishop I sat in the House of Lords as a 'Prelate', and then when I was made a life peer there was the question of my being reintroduced. To do that you need two supporters. I talked to Garter, King of Arms, and told him I had thought of asking Lord Runcie and Lord Cowdrey to be my supporters. He thought for a moment and said: 'Yes, God – and cricket. I think that would do very well.'

When Colin chaired the International Cricket Council, he gave himself an exhausting schedule, travelling the world. He liked to do business by personal conversation. He asked me if I thought it was still possible to speak of 'the spirit of the game'. I said I thought it could and should be. Colin fought for the way of playing hard but fair that makes up the spirit of the game. He was keen to see the 'code of practice' for cricketers adopted, that is now attached to the Laws of cricket.

He was a very warm friend to us. Like other friends of his, we would receive personal, handwritten notes of encouragement at special times in our lives. They meant a lot to us. On the 1962–63 tour there was a reception for the team and supporters. The hostess had organised the meal meticulously, so that everyone had to change tables after each course; she announced firmly: 'Nobody is to sit next to anybody they know.' Colin was in the middle of a conversation with my wife and said: 'We needn't take any notice of that, need we?' He was a warm person, very 'person-oriented', a conservative figure who loved traditions and fought for them. He was a man of integrity and of enthusiasm and of deep Christian faith. In his dealings with people he combined personal warmth with a keen attention to detail – a rare combination.

Michael Colin Cowdrey: b Ootacamund, India, 24 December 1932; d 4 December 200

7 MARCH 2005
THE RIGHT REVEREND LORD SHEPPARD OF LIVERPOOL
Batsman Who Followed Holy Orders

The Right Reverend the Lord Sheppard of Liverpool was an outstanding Bishop of Liverpool, particularly involved in the Church of England's social policies; earlier in his career he had been hardly less celebrated as the first ordained minister to have played Test cricket. Captain in turn of Cambridge and Sussex, Sheppard played for England before taking Orders. An opening batsman, he was at his prime during the three seasons from 1951 to 1953, in each of which he scored more than two thousand runs, compiling twenty-four centuries in the process. Once he started training for the priesthood in 1953, it seemed that his cricket would be confined to vacations. In the event, he would add the captaincy of England to his laurels, and make two centuries against Australia.

Those who regarded Sheppard as the epitome of polite, inoffensive Anglican respectability had some cause for surprise after he became Bishop of Liverpool in 1975. With his deep Biblical faith, and his commitment to social change, Sheppard proved a sharp critic of the Thatcher Government's policies – a stand that may have cost him the chance to succeed Robert Runcie as Archbishop of Canterbury.

The main elements of Sheppard the cricketer's game were already in place early on: sound defence, infinite patience, and an eagerness to drive off the front foot. Yet the start of his career at Sussex was a struggle. 'There are times,' he reflected, 'especially in big cricket, when it feels more like an ordeal by fire than a game.' Nevertheless he ended the 1949 season in a blaze of glory, with a double century and two centuries in successive matches. This promise was amply fulfilled in the next year, at Cambridge, where he held an exhibition to read history at Trinity Hall. He hit 227 against the West Indian tourists at Fenner's, and narrowly missed a century in the University Match when he was deceived by Donald Carr's googly on 93. Further solid performances for Sussex won him a place in the fourth Test against the West Indies; he made 11 and 29. During his second innings the birth of Princess Anne was announced. 'Let's have a wicket for the princess,' the West Indies responded, and Sheppard duly fell to Alf Valentine.

In 1950–51 he went with M.C.C. to Australia; with his high back-lift, however, he found it difficult to cope with the pace of Ray Lindwall and Keith Miller. He played in the last two Tests, battling to an honourable 41 in the second innings at Adelaide. Despite scoring heavily in 1951, Sheppard was unable to force his way into the England side. In 1952, however, his performances were almost Bradmanesque. As captain of Cambridge he hit seven centuries for the university, including 239 not out against Worcestershire (his highest first-class score), and 127 against Oxford in a drawn University Match. Recalled to the England side for the last two Tests against India in 1952, Sheppard made 119 at the Oval. He finished the season top of the first-class averages.

Sheppard had arrived at Cambridge with merely formal religious beliefs; then, during a Christian Union mission conducted by Dr Donald Grey Barnhouse, an American Evangelist, he underwent a conversion which gave him a deep and abiding Christian commitment. Even so, after deciding to prepare for ordination at Ridley Hall, he gave one last full season to Sussex in 1953, captaining them to second place in the championship. There was, however, no place for him in the England team who won back the Ashes that summer. Sheppard now imagined that his cricket would be restricted to the odd game for Sussex, as his ecclesiastical duties allowed. In 1954, however, he was approached by Ronnie Aird, secretary of M.C.C., who asked if he might be available to take on the England captaincy. England had just played a sour and bitter series in the West Indies, and the authorities were at that point wondering whether Hutton, for all his mastery as a batsman, was really the right man to lead his country. Sheppard decided that the situation warranted the interruption of his theological training, and agreed to make himself available for M.C.C.'s tour of Australia in 1954–55 if offered the captaincy. Early in June he returned to the Sussex side; and when Hutton fell ill after the first Test against Pakistan, he was duly called up to lead England in the second Test at Nottingham. England won by an innings, and Sheppard retained the captaincy for the next Test at Old Trafford, which was ruined by rain. Once again, he had proved himself a thoroughly competent leader; all the same it was finally decided that Hutton should captain England in Australia.

Sheppard professed relief, and went back to Ridley Hall prior to his ordination at Michaelmas 1955. He had managed, however, to play eighteen first-class matches that summer; and when, in June 1956, he made 97 for Sussex against the Australians, 'Gubby' Allen inquired whether he might be available for Test duty. Sheppard was allowed time off from his curacy to prepare himself for the role by playing for Sussex, and was quickly brought back to the England side for the fourth Test at Manchester.

This was the match in which Jim Laker took nineteen wickets; Sheppard, for his part, distinguished himself by scoring 113. He was equally impressive in the fifth Test at the Oval, when he made 62 on a bowlers' wicket.

In 1957 Sheppard was again recalled to the England side for the fourth and fifth Tests against the West Indies. That year, however, he was appointed warden of the Mayflower Family Centre in Canning Town, in East London, so that between 1958 and 1961 he was available to Sussex for only seven matches. This did not prevent him from again being touted as a potential England captain for the tour of Australia in 1962–63. In May 1962 Sheppard announced that he would play two months' cricket for Sussex. His performances were patchy, redeemed by a century for the Gentlemen against the Players at Lord's. Back in the England side for the fourth Test against Pakistan, he battled to 83, and then made another half-century at the Oval.

Ted Dexter, however, was appointed captain in Australia. Sheppard went as a member of the side, and secured an England victory with an innings of 113 not out at Melbourne. In the last Test, at Sydney, he made 68 and, by his own account, considered he had never batted better. Less happily, Sheppard, a fine fielder in his prime, dropped a number of catches in the series. 'It's a pity the Reverend don't put his hands together more often in the field,' Fred Trueman observed. On leave from his clerical duties, Sheppard refused to play on Sundays, though in those days this affected only charity matches. With the agreement of Ted Dexter and the Duke of Norfolk, the tour manager, he accepted invitations to preach in the cathedrals of all the Australian state capitals.

**David Stuart Sheppard: b Reigate, Surrey,
6 March 1929; d 5 March 2005**

30 APRIL 2007
LES JACKSON
'The Best Bowler in County Cricket'

Les Jackson played for Derbyshire from 1947 to 1963, and was revered by colleagues and opponents alike as one of the finest pacemen of his or any other day. 'County batsmen are inclined to talk more quietly or laugh a little louder at less funny jokes when they get near Derbyshire,' Ted Dexter observed. 'One name has been on their minds, the best bowler I faced – Les Jackson.' The ordeal was the worse because Cliff Gladwin would be operating in tandem from the other end. Don Bradman, who batted against him in 1948, the day after his 173 not out in the Headingley Test had won the Ashes for Australia, reckoned he was one of the best bowlers he encountered on that year's tour; Freddie Trueman rated him 'the best six-days-a-week bowler I saw in county cricket'. Tom Graveney remembered him as 'the best bloody bowler in the country', and confessed that he never felt at ease against him even when scoring runs. 'I used to finish up with bruises on the inside of both thighs,' he recalled. 'When I see Les socially nowadays I start rubbing the inside of my thighs.' Peter May, for his part, simply called Jackson 'magnificent'.

In his seventeen-year first-class career Jackson played in 418 matches and took 1,730 wickets at an average of 17.38. He claimed five wickets in an innings 115 times. The 13,867.5 overs he bowled each yielded an average of just over two runs, and nearly a third of them were maidens. And yet this universally admired bowler played only twice for England – against New Zealand at Old Trafford in 1949 and, twelve years later, in 1961, against Australia at Headingley. After both matches he was summarily dropped. On each occasion he had done well – in fact the seven wickets he took, at a typically economical 22.14 each, left him with a better Test average than any other England fast bowler between 1949 and 1961, saving only Trueman and Tyson.

Ted Dexter believed that Jackson's nagging accuracy in his Test against Australia in 1961 (his analyses were 31-11-52-2 and 13-5-26-2) helped assure England's eight-wicket victory. But apparently nothing he did impressed the selectors. Perhaps they attributed his achievements on the county circuit to the green Derbyshire pitches, which suited seam bowlers. Jackson confessed that he had no idea which direction the deliveries he bowled would move after they bounced. Batsmen were equally in the dark, aware only that the ball might come back or go away prodigious distances off the seam. But this did not happen merely at Chesterfield, Derby and Burton. Then again, purists objected to his action, complaining that his thirteen-pace run ended in a round-arm sling. It is true that Jackson's bowling looked ungainly, for he had never been coached as a boy. Yet it should have been results, not aesthetics, which counted with the selectors.

Another reason advanced for Jackson's omission from the England side was that his pace fell short of the fastest. This was true, but hardly relevant; indeed, Jackson was at his deadliest in 1958, when his pace was restricted by a groin strain. In any case, no one accused Jackson of lacking aggression. Ultimately, it is difficult to avoid the conclusion that Jackson's omission was partly due to snobbery. Derbyshire were an unfashionable county; Jackson was a coal miner. His biographer, Mike Carey, lays the blame at the door of Freddie Brown and Gubby Allen. Brown, who captained England between 1949 and 1951, apparently decided that Jackson lacked the stamina to come back for a second spell – a ludicrous criticism of a man who would bowl an average of 886 overs a season between 1949 and 1963.

Gubby Allen, an Old Etonian who played in twenty-five Tests but never took one hundred wickets in a season (a feat Jackson achieved ten times), was chairman of Test selectors from 1955 to 1961, when Jackson was at his peak. 'My information is,' Fred Trueman observed, 'that he [Allen] would not have Les at any price and if that's true it's criminal.' Even when Jackson played against the Australians in 1961, it was at Peter May's insistence. Tom Graveney, reflecting that another Old Etonian, R.W.V. Robins, played nineteen times for England against Jackson's twice, called this discrepancy 'sacrilege'. But Jackson himself never complained, either privately or in print. For him, playing cricket at any level was preferable to working in the pits.

Jackson was generally mild off the pitch and a fair, if hard, competitor on it. 'When he got you out,' Worcestershire's Martin Horton remembered, 'you never heard any snarling remarks or saw any gesture like you get from some of these prima donnas today.' He shared with Gladwin, however, a dislike of losing, and did not always take kindly to Donald Carr's efforts to force a victory through a sporting declaration. On one occasion, it is said, Jackson locked Carr out of the dressing room in order to prevent him getting on to the balcony to wave the batsmen in and close the innings.

Herbert Leslie Jackson: b Whitwell, Derbyshire, 5 April 1921; d 25 April 2007

2 JULY 2006
FRED TRUEMAN
Action Man Who was
the Greatest of the Great
Scyld Berry

When John Arlott was writing Fred Trueman's biography, he asked the Yorkshire and England bowler what the title should be. Trueman replied that it should be called the definitive biography of 't'finest bloody fast bowler that ever drew breath'. Trueman was not far out in his self-assessment. He was not the greatest bowler in terms of speed: when the sapient Australian Jack Fingleton first saw Trueman in 1953, when he was at his quickest, he thought Trueman's long run-up made him look faster than he was. He cannot be considered the greatest fast bowler of all time in terms of performance, either: that would have to be, if not one of his predecessors, then the Australian Dennis Lillee or the West Indian Malcolm Marshall. But from a visual point of view, Frederick Sewards Trueman, O.B.E., was and always will be the greatest.

Michael Holding had a beautiful bowling action, Harold Larwood too, but nobody has matched Trueman for a classical side-on action. It was magnificent theatre, and being no fool but full of street wisdom, coming as he did from a mining community, the man himself knew it. Fast bowlers of today, brought up in a sedentary lifestyle, have to train in the gym to build up their leg muscles. Fred's father was a miner at Stainton in South Yorkshire;

he himself left school at fourteen to work in a factory, and powerful legs – the basis of a fast bowler's work – came naturally.

As he walked back to his mark, Trueman would toss his mane of black hair, pivot on those legs of beef, and start his run-up. It was like a wave coming up the beach and crashing on to the shore, and something near a tidal wave at that. He did not run in a semicircle, but he did come in at an angle, leaning forward, gathering momentum, not tall but the embodiment of physical power. And the gracefulness of his run, by itself, would take the breath away. When Trueman reached the crease, his left arm was pointing towards the batsman as a veiled threat. When he lifted his left side into the air, his right arm was simultaneously cocked back, fully armed and ready to strike. The end-result was normally an outswinger to the right-handed batsman, if he had not been entranced by the spectacle which had unfolded before him.

In his youth, when he strained primarily for speed, Trueman was seen as the great white hope who could end the Australian supremacy which had existed since the Second World War. After making his first-class debut for Yorkshire in 1949, along with his future captain Brian Close, Trueman made his Test debut against India in 1952. He took eight wickets for thirty-one at Old Trafford, and helped to reduce India to nought for four at Headingley, the worst start in Test history. Close recalled that an Indian batsman asked the umpire to have a sightscreen moved. The umpire asked him where he wanted it: between me and the bowler, said the batsman.

'Trueman will get you' the Australian tourists were told by British servicemen on their voyage to England in 1953. It did not quite work out like that: it was Alec Bedser who got them with his medium-pace and inswing. But Trueman was released from National Service with the R.A.F. to play in the fifth Test at the Oval, and with four wickets for 86 did his part in the winning of the Ashes which crowned

Coronation year. For sheer speed Frank Tyson was Len Hutton's choice to go to Australia in 1954–55. There might have been some unruliness on Trueman's first tour of the West Indies the previous winter; in any event he did not make the trip to Australia. But he learnt meanwhile in county cricket, by bowling a thousand overs per season for Yorkshire and perfecting his craft as an outswing bowler who could also cut his pace down and bowl off-cutters.

The late 1950s and early 1960s were Trueman's boom period, when he became the celebrity 'Fiery Fred' and headed towards becoming the first bowler to take three hundred Test wickets. He succeeded Denis Compton as a Brylcreem boy, and was often pictured with a foaming pint in hand, though he was no beer-drinker, or else a pipe. The material rewards were not what they are today, and together with the lack of official recognition for his cricket wisdom, may have contributed to his curmudgeonliness in old age.

He was more effective at home than abroad. To this day nobody has taken more Test wickets in England than Trueman's 229, and in only forty-seven home Tests. He took seventy-eight Test wickets abroad because he only went on four tours, to the West Indies twice and to Australia and New Zealand twice. Those were the tours that mattered. If he had not spent so much energy on taking wickets – 2,304 of them in first-class cricket at eighteen runs each, making him the eighteenth leading wicket-taker of all time – he would have made a fine all-rounder. He scored over nine thousand first-class runs and three centuries. He was a brilliant fielder, too, mainly at short leg, where he had the strength and athleticism to squat after a long spell, when normal bowlers would have needed a winch to rise.

That he was a brilliant captain, too, if only on an occasional basis, was proved when he led Yorkshire to victory over the 1968 Australians at Bramall Lane: the tourists knew what they were up against, the 'sixth Test' they called it, but Trueman's Yorkshire still won handsomely. In his day fast bowlers were commonly supposed to be thick, but his shrewdness as a captain – then as a commentator on *Test Match Special* – began to alter public perceptions. When Tyson faded, Trueman gradually took over as England's strike bowler and inherited Brian Statham for a partner. The Lancastrian and the Yorkshireman made one of England's most famous pairs. Statham immaculate accuracy and steadiness, Trueman outswing and aggression: they did everything for England, except win the Ashes.

Trueman's finest series came in 1963, when he took thirty-four wickets in the five Tests against West Indies. He had everything then, speed and swing, combativeness and cunning. Pomp was a word used in frequent conjunction with Fred. Pomp with a hint of swagger. By the time the cameras were filming him in 1964, as he approached the unique number of three hundred Test wickets, Trueman had passed his peak. He was only thirty-three, but the heavy workload had taken its toll. It was a sedate outswinger, which the Australian Neil Hawke nicked to Colin Cowdrey at slip at the Oval in the final Test of the summer, that gave Trueman his three hundredth victim. 'Whoever does it will be bloody tired' was his comment when asked if his record would ever be overtaken.

Frederick Sewards Trueman: b Stainton, South Yorkshire, 6 February 1931; d 1 July 2006

12 JUNE 2000
BRIAN STATHAM
Modest Man from Modest Background
was True Great

Michael Henderson

Please excuse this intrusion into the death of a much-loved public performer but if I offer a private reflection on Brian Statham, it is because he played in the first cricket match I saw, and is one of the reasons I learnt to love the game. His passing is a reminder of how much has gone of life. A young boy growing up in Lancashire absorbed the greatness of 'George' Statham as he understood the huge public affection for Tom Finney or, in a different field, Kathleen Ferrier. It was a 'given'. Like them he came from a modest background and went on to conquer the world. Like them he never imagined that fame separated him from his fellows. Statham was approaching the end of his career when I first saw him bowl, against Derbyshire, in 1967. He was thirty-eight, a great age by today's standards, when he took six for 34 to bowl out Yorkshire for 61 a year later. So I can at least boast that I saw him run through the champions. That was his last fling. He retired at the end of the season and Fred Trueman, who played against him in that match, did not delay his own retirement long. Trueman and Statham: they went together like Lennon and McCartney, and it has been no surprise to hear the great Yorkshire bowler leading the tributes.

How far removed the lion-hearted Statham was from the world

of players trotting off to see psychologists 'to get their minds right'! The abiding image of this lean, wiry man with the double-jointed action was of a fast bowler who ran in, rain or shine, and took his pleasures in the saloon bar with a fag or two and several pints of bitter, or mild. He wasn't choosy. Times change quickly, and reputations fade. The generation growing up today may not be familiar with men like Statham. Indeed, on England's tour of South Africa last winter, one (admittedly young) member of the party failed to recognise Colin Cowdrey in a group portrait. Laugh if you like, but it's true.

Players can be unreceptive to the achievements of the past. David Green, who grew up under Statham at Old Trafford and who writes about cricket for this paper, was once talking to a young English bowler who took a dim view of previous generations, and wondered, in particular, whether Statham was fast. 'How fast do you think he was, then?' Green asked. 'About as sharp as Neil Foster,' was the reply. 'I'll tell you how fast he was,' said Greeny. 'Roy Marshall reckoned that if he could push George through mid-off for a couple in his fifth over he was doing pretty well. And Roy Marshall could play a bit. Ne'then, lad, shall we look at your figures?' That chastened young shaver, incidentally, never played for England. Statham did, seventy times, and took 252 wickets, often with Trueman at the other end. Whereas Trueman was fast and, on occasions, wild, Statham was the model of accuracy, operating on the premise of 'you miss, I hit'. As Neville Cardus wrote: 'Did Statham ever send down a wide?'

There were times when he came off the field with blood in his boots but, privately and publicly, there were no grumbles. He belonged to a generation who had seen real hardship at first hand and such experience tends to put things like cricket into a clearer perspective. How high does he stand in the pantheon? Pretty near the top. Besides Trueman, only Ian Botham, Bob Willis and Derek Underwood have taken more Test wickets for England. Of the eighteen bowlers who have exceeded Statham's aggregate of 2,260 first-class wickets, none took them more cheaply than he did, at 16.37. For Lancashire he stands shoulder to shoulder with Cyril Washbrook as the club's most distinguished player. He took 1,816 wickets for the county at the barely believable average of 15.12.

When one considers the longevity of his career, and the peaks he scaled along the way, nobody can question his claim to greatness, though this modest man would never press his own case. Statham brought to the game that most precious of human qualities: glory, lightly worn. He added a verse to the eternal chorus, and must be remembered.

**John Brian Statham: b Gorton, Manchester,
17 June 1930; d 10 June 2000**

29 SEPTEMBER 2007
DEREK SHACKLETON
Last in a Line of England Aces
David Green

Derek Shackleton was one of the last of a great line of English medium-pacers. Shack was an easy-going man who took one hundred wickets in a season twenty times, a number exceeded only by Wilfred Rhodes and matched by no one else in the game's long history. During his twenty-one-year Hampshire career, Shackleton played seven Tests for England, but they were contained in two separate series a decade apart. In 1963 he took seven wickets in the Lord's Test against the West Indies but will be remembered for his run-out which brought the injured Colin Cowdrey to the crease to see out a draw.

It is fashionable now to dismiss men like Shackleton as 'automatic bowlers'. So 'automatic' was Shack that he bowled as perfect a length, too. Shack's movement through the air was generally away from the right-hander, though he occasionally bowled an inswinger. And so perfect was his action, it hit the bat near the splice.

During my chequered career I made two 'pairs', one against Shack at Old Trafford in 1962. First innings: nip-backer caught at short leg. Second innings: bounced and left me, caught off the bat's shoulder by second slip running back. Helpless both times. Ted Dexter told me how Sussex, wearying of blocking Shack, decided to slog him. 'We were all caught off strange parts of the bat,' he said.

'Shack still got six-for, but in twelve overs rather than the usual twenty-eight.'

About 1,200 overs a season was routine for him and I can't remember him breaking down. He was slim and lithe and his action was easy, which enabled him to get through an immense amount of work. In 1961, when Hampshire won the championship for the first time, he bowled 1,501.5 overs, taking 158 wickets at 19. All done without breaking sweat.

Derek Shackleton: b Todmorden, West Yorkshire, 12 August 1924; d 28 September 2007

5 AUGUST 2008
BUTCH WHITE
The Bowler at the Other End
to Shackleton

Butch White played a crucial part in securing Hampshire's first championship title in 1961. At that time many, if not Fred Trueman, thought him the fastest bowler in England. Some pacemen – Brian Statham, Michael Holding, Glenn McGrath – have been rangy, supple creatures who combined menace with athletic grace. Others – Frank Tyson, Wes Hall, Jeff Thomson – have been obvious tough guys, ostentatiously determined to batter opponents into submission. Butch White belonged very much to the second category: a bundle of muscle, he ran in to bowl from a twenty-five-yard run with fierce, bustling and uncompromising energy, clearly bent on wreaking havoc. His delivery stride, in John Arlott's phrase, was 'a mighty, convulsive heave'. Many county batsmen devoutly wished themselves at the other end, save that – and here lay the nub of Hampshire's success in 1961 – at the other end they encountered Derek Shackleton, one of the supreme medium-pace bowlers of all time.

Sour Yorkshiremen still whinge that Hampshire's championship triumph that summer depended on generous declarations by other southern counties. The facts, however, do not support them. Hampshire carried off the title because the captain, Colin

Ingleby-Mackenzie, was justified in his confidence that his bowlers could dismiss the opposition twice. If the principal honours must go to Shackleton, who took 153 county championship wickets in 1961, it should not be forgotten that White captured 117.

Always given to unpredictable streaks of brilliance, White brought off a particularly memorable performance that August, against Sussex at Portsmouth. On the evening of the second day Sussex, with Jim Parks and Ted Dexter at the crease, were 179 for four in their second innings, 141 ahead, and seemingly in a position to set Hampshire a challenging target on the morrow. 'Give me just one over, Butch, would you?' Ingleby-Mackenzie asked. White, who up to that point in the match had bowled with scant success, took a hat-trick with his first three balls, and with his fourth saw the new batsman dropped by Jimmy Gray at slip. The fifth ball passed without incident; off the sixth White claimed another victim, caught in the gully. Sussex were all out for 180, and Hampshire won by six wickets. Jimmy Gray attempted an apology for his dropped catch. 'No more than I'd expect,' returned White, who liked to project the image of a fierce and grumpy fast bowler. In fact, he was one of the most popular players in county cricket.

White bowled his heart out at all times, and only wished that he could have produced his all-conquering phases at will. Some suggested that they tended to occur when the pressure was off. 'I can remember the Test selectors watching, and he'd bowl at medium pace,' recalled Bryan Timms, Hampshire's wicketkeeper. 'If you came back that afternoon when they'd gone, he'd be on fire.' A left-handed batsman – he bowled right-handed – and very much a tail-ender, White favoured the agricultural in his shot selection. Once every blue moon this method produced sensational results. Against Oxford University, in 1960, he plundered twenty-eight off an over from the off-spinner Dan Piachaud: 0, 6, 6, 6, 6, 4. Much more important was White's innings against Gloucestershire at Portsmouth in June 1961, as the championship race was developing. Hampshire, chasing a total of 199, seemed likely to lose at 162 for eight. White, however, marched in and to general consternation secured a crucial victory with a speedy 33 not out.

The contribution of White's bowling towards Hampshire's title was recognised by his selection for the tour of Pakistan and India in 1961–62. He played in the first Test against Pakistan at Lahore in October, and quickly dismissed the openers, Hanif Mohammad and Imtiaz Ahmed. At the end of the innings he had the respectable figures of three for 65. For most of the tour, however, he was plagued with injury, perhaps a delayed effect of his efforts over the previous two English summers. In 1961, for instance, he bowled 1,010 overs, as compared with Matthew Hoggard's 277 and Steve Harmison's 363 in the first-class averages of 2007. White kept fit by running in Army boots during the winter, and, as he insisted, simply by bowling during the summer. Yet in Pakistan and India he proved more fragile than in England, which was all the more serious because, astonishingly, the touring party did not include a phsyiotherapist.

Though White comfortably headed the tourists' bowling averages with thirty-two wickets at 19.84 apiece (including one match, against a Services side, in which he took four wickets in five balls), he played in only one other Test, against Pakistan at Karachi in February 1962. On that occasion he broke down after sixteen balls and one wicket. It was a severe disappointment to White that he was never given another chance. The supreme moment of his career remained the day that Hampshire clinched the championship. 'I came along next morning,' recalled team-mate Alan Castell, 'and the first thing I saw was Butch White's car, parked on its own right in the middle of the road. He'd got so pissed someone had to take him home.'

David William White: b Sutton Coldfield, Warwickshire, 14 December 1935; d 1 August 2008

15 MARCH 2006
COLIN INGLEBY-MACKENZIE
The Captain Who Played for Fun

Colin Ingleby-Mackenzie led Hampshire to victory in the county championship of 1961 with unforgettable flair and panache, and was later president of M.C.C. His daredevil image became fixed in the public consciousness through reports of a television interview he gave on *Junior Sportsview*. His earnest, po-faced interlocutor clearly knew nothing about cricket, and Ingleby-Mackenzie could not resist the temptation to send him up. Their exchange lives in the memory:

'Mr Ingleby-Mackenzie, to what do you attribute Hampshire's success?'
'Oh, wine, women and song, I should say.'
'But don't you have certain rules, discipline, helpful hints for the younger viewer?'
'Well, everyone in bed in time for breakfast, I suppose.'
'Yes, thank you. Perhaps we could take a look in the dressing room?'
'Certainly, if you don't mind me wandering about in the nude.'

There was, of course, a great deal more to Ingleby-Mackenzie's captaincy than he cared to suggest in that interview. He was able to demonstrate by example what so many professional cricketers are inclined to forget: that cricket should be played for fun, as well as for victory. Under his command the Hampshire dressing room echoed with laughter, and it did no harm to morale that the captain attracted a string of women visitors. While there was no lack of stern intent, cheerfulness kept breaking through, helping to take the pressure off the players, who were made aware that life afforded concerns other than cricket. He once persuaded the umpire Harry Baldwin to bring a wireless on to the field so that he could listen to an important horse race.

Another much-quoted example of his jocular approach came in 1956 when Ingleby-Mackenzie went on a tour to the West Indies organised by Jim Swanton. He knew exactly how to treat the *Telegraph's* august cricket correspondent, who loved to be teased – at least by dashing young Etonians. Ingleby-Mackenzie professed bafflement when Swanton insisted that the players should be in bed by 11. 'But surely,' he objected, 'the match starts at 11.30.'

The captain was not just universally liked; he inspired trust and loyalty. His players sensed the deep kindness and loyalty that lay beneath the jokiness and bravado, and drew confidence from knowing how he hated dropping someone from the team. If he made mistakes, they were never dictated by meanness, spite or arrogance. As for tactics, Ingleby-Mackenzie disclaimed all knowledge. 'Roy Marshall and Leo Harrison do all that,' he explained. Where Ingleby-Mackenzie excelled, as became an *aficionado* of the Turf, was in his love of risk and his skill in calculating the odds. The essential element in Hampshire winning the championship in 1961 was their ability to bowl sides out twice. But Ingleby-Mackenzie's brilliantly calculated declarations again and again opened up prospects of victory in a summer when the follow-on was not allowed. No fewer than ten of Hampshire's nineteen victories were achieved in this way.

Another critical factor was the captain's ability to rise to the occasion with the bat. An aggressive left-hander with a marvellous eye, Ingleby-Mackenzie disdained any attempt at consistency and became increasingly addicted to the cross-batted slog. Thus the statistics of his 343 matches in first-class cricket between 1951 and 1965 – 12,421 runs (eleven centuries) at an average of 24.35 – do no justice to his talent. He did, however, have the knack of catching fire at critical moments. Perhaps his greatest innings came at a key point in the struggle for the championship in 1961 when he murdered the Essex attack at Cowes, scoring 132 not out in 140 minutes to secure a crucial victory. He might have made a fine captain of England, though he always insisted that he was not good enough to play Test cricket. It is true that he did not possess tunnel vision, or the desire to be taken seriously. Yet it was precisely because he was not totally consumed by the game – cynics would note his susceptibility to injury in Ascot week – that he was able to create the atmosphere in which 'Happy Hants' triumphed.

Alexander Colin David Ingleby-Mackenzie:
b Dartmouth, Devon, 15 September 1933; d 9 March 2006

10 JULY 2008
BRYAN 'BOMBER' WELLS
The Cricketer as an Eccentric

Bryan 'Bomber' Wells, an off-spin bowler for Gloucestershire and Nottinghamshire, was one of the funniest and most eccentric county cricketers of the 1950s and 1960s. Overweight and undertrained, Bomber Wells could hardly have looked less like a professional sportsman. This unathletic impression was confirmed by his bowling run-up, or rather his lack of run-up. As he himself explained, he took two steps when he was cold and one when he was hot; and sometimes he simply delivered the ball from a stationary position. Once at Worcester, by pre-arrangement with Roly Jenkins, who was batting, Wells managed to bowl an entire over while the cathedral clock struck twelve. Sir Derrick Bailey, 3rd Baronet, the Gloucestershire captain, was furious, and complained to Wells that he was making the game look ridiculous. Bomber was ordered to start his run from eight paces back. He obeyed but then bowled the ball – spot on to a length – after taking only a couple of paces. 'Sir Derrick went berserk,' Bomber recalled with satisfaction. 'He dropped me for two matches, but it was worth it.'

Inevitably, many batsmen were unprepared for Bomber's delivery. Playing as a young man for the Gloucestershire Nondescripts against Witney, he bowled out a batsman called Len Hemming, who was immediately called back as he had not seemed to be ready. With the next ball Bomber bowled him out again. 'If you think I'm staying here for him to get his bloody hat-trick,' Hemming told the fielders, 'you've got another think coming.' Years later Hemming was asked about this story. 'I've no recollection of it at all,' he said, 'but I'm all in favour of it.' Playing against Essex in the county championship, Wells encountered a young amateur who stepped away from the crease whenever he began to bowl. So, in Bomber's own words, 'I ran all the way round the square, past mid-on, square leg, behind the 'keeper, back to mid-off, and I shouted, "Are you ready now?" And I bowled him first ball.' These, and many other stories about Bomber Wells are to be found in Stephen Chalke's wonderfully evocative memoir, *One More Run* (2000). The book also makes it clear, however, that Bomber Wells was a very fine bowler.

Oddly for such a thickset man, he had small hands, and seemed to spin the ball from the palm rather than the fingers. 'He was the only bowler I've ever seen,' remembered his Gloucestershire colleague Arthur Milton, 'who made the ball pitch further up to you than it looked. He had such a quick arm action that the ball would be on you, half a yard further up than you thought.' Many batsmen were trapped lbw on the back foot. It was Wells's misfortune, though, that in his time Gloucestershire had two other fine off-spinners in John Mortimore and David Allen, both of whom played for England. In order to be sure of regular county championship cricket Wells moved to Nottinghamshire in 1960. Yet his bowling average for Gloucestershire – 544 wickets at 21.18 each – was better than either Mortimore's (1,696 wickets at 22.69) or Allen's (882 wickets at 22.13). Many county cricketers, including so hardened a professional as Brian Close, felt that Wells's unpredictability made him the most dangerous of the three. He was always changing his pace, and would mix off-spin with away swingers and leg-breaks. 'It used to bore me silly to bowl two balls the same,' he said. What counted against him in some eyes was his inability to be anything but his own man, or to play the game for any other reason but enjoyment. A man capable, during tense moments on the field, of creeping up behind his fiercely disciplinarian county captain George Emmett and saying 'Boo', was never going to be entirely acceptable in the grim grind of professional cricket.

His attitude to batting never changed. He had one shot – the slog. 'If I hit the ball,' Bomber explained, 'it went a long way and the crowd and I were happy. If I missed it, well, I was that much nearer bowling.' Team-mates were frequently driven to fury by his running between the wickets. 'Can't you say anything?' Sam Cook once shouted, stranded in mid-pitch by Bomber's failure to call. 'Goodbye,' Bomber volunteered.

Wells made his debut for Gloucestershire against Sussex at Bristol, and Sir Derrick Bailey evidently did not have much confidence in the newcomer, for Bomber came on as sixth change bowler. Almost immediately, however, he claimed his first victim, David Sheppard, the future Bishop of Liverpool. At the end of the innings his figures were six for 47. 'Well,' he told his new teammates in the pavilion, 'I can see if I'm going to play for this side, I'm going to have to do a lot of bowling. I shall have to cut my run down.'

Many counselled against the move to Nottinghamshire, arguing that the wicket at Trent Bridge was too favourable to batsmen. But Bomber found he preferred it to the slower pitches at Bristol; he also preferred the food at Trent Bridge, finding it a great advance on 'the little salads we used to have every day at Bristol: one slice of cold meat so thin you could see through it'. Eating, he confessed, was his second pastime.

Wells retired in 1965, having taken, as he was told, 999 wickets in 302 first-class matches. Offered a game against Gloucestershire to make up the thousand – 'somebody down there will give you their wicket' – he demurred. 'Plenty of people have got a thousand wickets,' he reflected, 'I bet no one's got 999.' Later, however, it was discovered he had only taken 998.

**Bryan Douglas Wells: b Gloucester, 27 July 1930;
d 19 June 2008**

30 NOVEMBER 2004
BILL ALLEY
The Tough Aussie with a Liking for
Theatrical Displays

Bill Alley was an Australian cricketer with a formidable record in the Lancashire League when in 1957, already thirty-eight, he signed a contract to play for Somerset. The county must have hoped to get perhaps five years' service from him. In the event, Alley would be the mainstay of the Somerset side for twelve seasons, performing extraordinary feats with both bat and ball, and pulling in the crowds with his rumbustious, aggressive style.

A left-handed batsman, Alley believed that the ball was there to be hit, and set about the task with a wonderful eye and an extravagant lack of classical technique. Straight deliveries might be chopped down to third man, while good length balls outside the off stump would frequently be dispatched to leg. No matter how many fielders were placed between square leg and long on, he possessed the power to slog the ball either between them or over them. Then, having driven the connoisseurs of style into despair, he would suddenly unfurl a perfect cover drive, as if to show that he could play that way, too, when the mood took him. As a right-arm medium-fast bowler, Alley presented a far more niggardly persona, resenting every run conceded, and combining great accuracy with an ability to move the ball both in the air and off the seam.

His best seasons were 1961 and 1962. In 1961 he scored 3,019 runs (he remains the last person to score more than three thousand runs in an English summer) and took sixty-two wickets. In one golden patch he hit 523 runs in eight days for once out. Against Surrey he scored 183, 134, 150 and nine without being dismissed. Altogether he made eleven centuries in 1961, and was particularly pleased that two of them, and another innings of 95, came against the Australians. 'Their flabby bowling almost made me want to weep,' he declared with ill-concealed delight. 'The Don wouldn't have stood for such mediocrity.' In 1962 Alley did the double, with 1,915 runs and 112 wickets. The combination of his hard-hitting batting and thrifty bowling also made him a particularly useful player in the new one-day game. In 1967 he helped guide Somerset to the final of the Gillette Cup, though they lost to Kent at Lord's.

It was hinted to Alley, then playing for New South Wales, that he would be chosen for the tour of England in 1948. Around this time, however, he suffered a terrible accident when Jock Livingston (later of Northamptonshire), playing in a net alongside, hit a full-blooded hook shot which came through the netting and hit him flush on the left side of the jaw. Alley was unconscious for sixteen hours, and his jaw had to be re-constructed and sewn up with sixty stitches. The accident put paid to his boxing career (he had twenty-eight professional fights at welterweight, and won every one of them), and for a while even his future as a cricketer seemed in doubt.

On and off the pitch Alley was a tough, highly talkative competitor, very much in the Australian mould. It would not be altogether fair to pillory him for sledging, for he was fundamentally too good-humoured to be really vicious. In Fred Trueman, however, he found a worthy sparring mate. Alley set the tone on the first occasion he faced the great fast bowler, in 1957. 'For two overs we exchanged scowl for scowl. Then, loudly enough for Fred to hear, I said to Paddy Corrall, one of the umpires, "I thought this cock was quick. When's he going to let one go?"' Alley remembered another time when he drove Trueman's first ball and hooked the next to the boundary – 'a gesture tantamount to tickling a bush snake. Fred reacted with two bumpers, the crowd booed, and at the end of the over I set them off again by striding down the pitch with bat raised. Fred played along by striding out to meet me halfway. Suddenly the fans grew very quiet as they saw Fred push his face into mine. And out of the corner of his mouth came the promise, "First pint's on me tonight, Bill".'

Alley loved such theatrical displays. His pranks, though, were not always innocent. Once at Bournemouth he borrowed the umpire's penknife, and began without any attempt at concealment to cut round the new ball, lifting the seam in the process. The umpire, outraged, spoke of reporting him to Lord's. 'You'd look nice,' Alley returned, 'after giving me the knife and standing by my side while I picked the seam.' Nothing more was heard of the matter.

William Edward Alley: b Hornsby, Sydney, New South Wales, 3 February 1919; d 26 November 2004

8 APRIL 2005
KEN SUTTLE
Loyal Servant with an Infectious
Sense of Fun

Ken Suttle was a prolific left-handed batsman for Sussex; his most remarkable feat, however, was to set a record of 423 consecutive appearances in county championship matches. This achievement, spread over fifteen years between August 1954 and July 1969, was the more remarkable in that Sussex at that period readily left out proven professionals in order to accommodate brilliant occasional amateurs such as David Sheppard, Hubert Doggart and the Nawab of Pataudi. Suttle's batting was simply too good to be denied. Short in stature, he combined a wonderful eye with a quick-footed adaptability which enabled him to excel with the pull, the cut and the glance. And though he did not take a wicket in his first seven seasons with Sussex, in 1956 he suddenly emerged as a dangerous occasional left-arm spinner, heading the county bowling averages that year with twenty-four victims at 16.75 apiece.

Suttle's confident, chirpy manner and his infectious sense of fun endeared him to everyone connected with Sussex cricket. No matter how formidable the bowler, Suttle was always convinced that he had his measure, and he became one of the select band who scored more than thirty thousand runs in first-class cricket. In addition, his fleet athleticism made him a brilliant fielder. Ever eager, he liked to change positions frequently in order to find a new audience for his irrepressible chatter. Like his Sussex predecessor John Langridge, Suttle was unfortunate not to play for England. He did well on M.C.C.'s tour of the West Indies in 1953–54, averaging 41.83 with the bat. After top-scoring in both innings with scores of 96 and 62 against Barbados just before the second Test, he might have expected to win an England cap. The last batting place, however, went to the player-manager, Charles Palmer.

For the rest of his career Suttle's talents were devoted to Sussex. His astonishing run of appearances in the county championship reflected not only his fitness, but also his courage in making light of injury. His friend Alan Oakman remembers batting with Suttle in 1963 against Charlie Griffith, the fearsome West Indian fast bowler. Suttle was struck in the face and shed masses of blood, but insisted on carrying on. Three years later, in the same fixture, Griffith once more reduced Suttle's face to a bloody wreck. Oakman, again at the bowler's end, went down the pitch to ask the victim if he was all right. 'Oh yes,' came the reply, 'he's not as fast as he was.'

He was awarded his county cap in 1952, when he topped one thousand runs for the first of seventeen times, and saved a match against Worcestershire with a brilliant maiden century in only ninety-five minutes. On that occasion he put on 119 for the eighth wicket with a former Cambridge Blue called Kelland, whose contribution was only five. Suttle's final total of 29,375 runs for Sussex puts him second in the list of run-scorers for the county, after John Langridge. He played 601 times for the county, a number exceeded only by Langridge (622 matches) and George Cox senior (618).

Suttle was unlucky that one-day cricket, to which he was particularly suited, was introduced only when his career was well advanced. His crisp batting and his ability to throw on the turn in the field played an important part in Sussex's winning the Gillette Cup in both 1963 and 1964, the first two years of the competition. When Mike Griffith, the captain of Sussex in 1969, telephoned Suttle to tell him that, after 423 consecutive county championship games, he would be omitted from the side to play Surrey at the Oval early in August, the news was not well received. 'Christ,' Griffith reported, 'he wanted to know why ten other buggers hadn't been left out before him.' Later that month Suttle underlined his point with a century against Middlesex.

The end of Suttle's long and distinguished career was callously handled. He turned up at the beginning of the 1971 season only to be informed he would not be needed – ever again. In fact he did play a few matches that summer, but was relegated to the second XI in 1972, when he shared a benefit with Jim Parks. The episode recalled Sussex's appalling treatment of Maurice Tate, their greatest bowler, who was summarily dismissed in 1937 after a quarter of a century of strenuous service.

Kenneth George Suttle: b Hammersmith, West London, 25 August 1928; d 25 March 2005

23 SEPTEMBER 2011
THE NAWAB OF PATAUDI
Batsman Who Overcame His Handicap

The Nawab of Pataudi captained India in forty Test matches and scored six Test centuries – all despite having only one functioning eye. He had seemed destined to become a batsman of supreme distinction. But on 1 July 1961, as a passenger in a car accident, his right eye was pierced by a shard of glass from the windscreen. Inevitably this made it difficult for Pataudi to judge the length of the bowling he faced. His plight was made worse because he had always relied rather more on instinct than technique. Immediately, though, he undertook the challenge of rebuilding his career. After four months of concentrated experiment in the nets, he accepted an invitation to captain the Indian Board President's XI against Ted Dexter's M.C.C. team in Hyderabad. When Pataudi went in to bat, with a contact lens in his near-sightless right eye, he found he was seeing two balls, six or seven inches apart. By picking the inner one, he managed to reach 35. At this point he removed the contact lens, and, keeping the bad eye closed, succeeded in taking his score to 70.

A month later, in December 1961, he made his Test debut for India against England in Delhi. In his first four Test innings he registered scores of 13, 64, 32 and 103 (the latter in only 140 minutes), contributing largely to India's first victory in a series against England. This was a truly heroic achievement. By the end of the season Pataudi reckoned that he had discovered the best means of overcoming his handicap, pulling the peak of his cap over his right eye to eliminate the blurred double image he otherwise saw. He still had difficulty, though, in judging flight against slow bowlers. Inevitably, genius lost something to caution and orthodoxy.

Naturally, his record begs the question of what he might have achieved with two good eyes. Yet Pataudi never made excuses, or indulged in self pity. In his autobiography, *Tiger's Tale* (1969), he admitted simply that he had had to abandon his early ambition of becoming one of the greatest batsmen. Instead, he wrote: 'I have concentrated on trying to make myself a useful one, and a better fielder than my father was.'

The son of the eighth Nawab of Pataudi, he was born Mohamed Mansur Ali Khan and grew up in a palace boasting 150 rooms, run by well over one hundred servants – eight of whom were employed as personal attendants to the son and heir, known from infancy as 'Tiger'. His father was a talented cricketer in his own right, and played for England against Australia on the tour of 1932–33, making a century on his Test debut in Sydney. Though plagued by ill health, he became one of the very few cricketers to play for two countries when he captained the Indians in England in 1946. Whereas Pataudi senior had been known for the elegance and delicacy of his stroke play, his son transcended classical style, relying at this early stage on eagle eyes that enabled him to get away with the slashing cut and the cross-batted pull, even against bowling which seemed to demand respect. His father died in 1952, aged only forty-one, so that Tiger, aged eleven, became the ninth Nawab of Pataudi.

In 1961, Pataudi, captain of Oxford, reached his absolute peak. Against the full Yorkshire attack, which included four England bowlers, he scored 106 and 103 not out. When he turned Trueman, who was bowling at full pace, off his stumps for four down to long leg, the Yorkshire champion raised his hand in salute. By the end of June, with three games still to play, Pataudi was only ninety-two runs short of his father's record total of 1,307 runs in an Oxford season. Then came the accident in Hove.

Mohamed Mansur Ali Khan: b Bhopal, 5 January 1941; d 22 September 2011

28 FEBRUARY 2004

JACK FLAVELL
Bowler who Took No Prisoners

Jack Flavell was a formidable fast bowler for Worcestershire in the 1950s and 1960s; it was largely owing to the opening attack he formed with Len Coldwell, and to the batting of Tom Graveney, that the county won their first championship title in 1964, and repeated the triumph the next season. Graveney believed that Flavell and Coldwell, when both fully fit, were the most hostile pair of fast bowlers he saw in county cricket. Flavell, in particular, took no prisoners. In those days, before helmets were part of a batsman's armoury, there were stories of tail-enders hiding in the lavatories at the prospect of facing him on a fast wicket.

When the sixteen-year-old Nawab of Pataudi, a Winchester schoolboy, played his first game for Sussex in August 1957, Flavell lost no time in bouncing him out for a duck. In the second innings, Pataudi, ready for what was coming, ducked, leaving his bat in the air. The ball struck it and rocketed down to third man for four, his first runs in senior cricket. The next year, Flavell was unwise enough to bowl a short delivery which hit Les Jackson, the deadly Derbyshire fast bowler. The Worcestershire fielders winced at the vengeance to come – and still more at the treatment accorded them when they reached the crease. Flavell, however, was not required to bat.

Fortunately for batsmen, both Flavell and Coldwell were liable to strains, which sometimes forced them to bowl within themselves. Yet the red-haired, red-faced Flavell was immensely strong and powerful, and never more dangerous than when coming back after injury. He had been unable to bowl for a period in 1964, and Worcestershire's championship hopes appeared to be slipping when they recorded only one win in six matches. Flavell, however, stormed back and in five matches between 8 and 25 August took forty-six wickets at only 11.71 apiece, including one analysis of nine for 56 against Middlesex. Against Nottinghamshire he even put in a rare performance with the bat, striking two fours to secure a one-wicket victory. In the end, Worcestershire won the title by forty-one points, with Flavell claiming 101 wickets for them.

Next year, 1965, Flavell was available for all twenty-eight championship matches, and again played a crucial role as Worcestershire, after a bad start, won ten of their last eleven games to squeak home in front of Northamptonshire. Flavell's contribution to this second title was 132 wickets at only 14.99 apiece. His superb form continued in 1966, when he finished second in the first-class averages with 135 wickets at an average of 14.00. But for adverse weather, Worcestershire might well have won a third successive title.

Flavell's best year was 1961, which he finished as the country's leading bowler, with 171 victims. Called up for the bowling attack in the fourth Test against Australia at Headingley, he claimed two prize scalps in Bobby Simpson and Peter Burge. But Australia, having been well behind on first innings, turned the game with a last-wicket partnership of ninety-eight in their second innings. The England captain, Peter May, was much criticised for persisting too long with his spinners; certainly when he finally brought back Flavell, the stand was instantly broken. But the breakthrough came too late, for Benaud was able to exploit the rough outside the leg stump to bowl Australia to victory by fifty-four runs.

Flavell played again at the Oval, accounting for Neil Harvey and Ken 'Slasher' Mackay, but was then ignored by the selectors until 1964. Early that season Ted Dexter, the England captain, had a very rough time facing Flavell and Coldwell in a county match, and wanted to see the Australians endure a similar torture. Both Worcestershire fast bowlers were called up for the first Test at Trent Bridge, and with considerable help from Fred Trueman on a rain-affected pitch they shot out the Australians for 168. Flavell missed the second Test, and in the third was unable to make any impression on a good batting wicket at Headingley. He broke down with a strained Achilles tendon and never played for England again, rather to the relief of Worcestershire supporters, who were keen to have him in the county attack at all times. Team-mates, meanwhile, found him a competitive whist player, given to throwing the pack out of the coach window when the cards ran against him.

John Alfred Flavell: b Wall Heath, Staffordshire, 15 May 1929; d 25 February 2004

23 NOVEMBER 2006
GEOFF GRIFFIN
Fast Bowler Bedevilled by
'Throwing' Controversy

Geoff Griffin, the South African fast bowler, remains the only player to have taken a hat-trick in a Test at Lord's; his international career, however, was extinguished during that same match in June 1960, when he was no-balled eleven times for throwing. This was a climactic incident in a controversy which has haunted cricket since overarm bowling was legalised in 1864. It is easy enough to pronounce that the elbow joint should not be straightened in the delivery of the ball; far harder to decide with certainty when this rule has been infringed.

South Africa were undeniably taking a chance in including among their side in 1960 a bowler who had been no-balled for throwing the previous winter, when playing for Natal. In May 1960, playing against M.C.C. at Lord's, Griffin was called for throwing on eight occasions, the first time this had happened to a touring player; and soon afterwards his action was again penalised in a match against Nottinghamshire. A three-day session in the nets under the expert tuition of Alf Gover seemed to have helped, but at the cost of rendering Griffin less effective as a strike force. Even so, he took four wickets in the first Test at Edgbaston (during which he celebrated his twenty-first birthday), apparently without offending the umpires.

Nevertheless, eyebrows were raised when he strained for more pace at the end of the first day, and a week later he was once more called for throwing in the South Africans' match against Hampshire.

In the second Test at Lord's Griffin's troubles began in the third over, when he was no-balled by umpire Frank Lee, at square leg. Though he soon claimed the wicket of Colin Cowdrey, he received four more calls for throwing that day. Some spectators were puzzled because they could scarcely discern any difference in his action between one ball and another: the feeling was that either all, or none, of his deliveries should have been called. On the second day Griffin was given the new ball after lunch, and no-balled on his fifth and sixth deliveries, again by Lee from square leg. Lee allowed the next delivery; this time, though, Griffin was called for dragging by Syd Buller at the bowler's end. Remarkably, he kept up his spirits, and maintained considerable hostility. Towards the end of the day he had M.J.K. Smith caught behind off the last ball of an over, and then bowled Peter Walker and Fred Trueman with the first two balls of the next over. It was the first hat-trick claimed by South Africa in Test cricket.

South Africa were twice dismissed cheaply, and lost by an innings shortly after lunch on the fourth day. Since the Queen was due to visit Lord's at tea-time, an exhibition match was arranged to fill in the time. Though Griffin bowled at half-pace, he was again judged to be throwing, this time by Buller at square leg. Cruelly, when he switched to underarm in order to finish the over, he was no-balled by Lee for not informing him of his change of action. Afterwards, Griffin remembered, Don Bradman appeared in the South Africans' dressing room to commiserate, and told him that the umpires were acting under orders from Gubby Allen.

Far from clarifying the matter, modern technology – capable of 1,000 frames per second – has merely established that pretty well every bowler flexes his arm in the act of delivery. So in 2005 it was decreed that fifteen degrees of elbow bend should be allowed. Who knows what the cameras might have decided in the case of Griffin, who had suffered an accident at school which left him with a permanent crook in the right elbow, and an incapacity to straighten his arm?

After the Lord's Test in 1960, Griffin did not bowl again on tour, though he played as a batsman, making some useful scores at number nine. He won universal praise for the calm, philosophical manner with which he confronted misfortune. He played for Rhodesia in 1961–62 and 1962–63, but the experience of being repeatedly no-balled in a match against North-Eastern Transvaal in Salisbury finished him off as a first-class cricketer, aged just twenty-three. Employed by South African Breweries in his cricketing heyday, he subsequently became a hotel manager for them, first at the Argyll, and then at the Congela Hotel in Durban. His crooked right arm continued to be a liability. When he challenged some visitors to his hotel to arm-wrestling, his very first opponent broke his arm.

Geoffrey Merton Griffin: b Greytown, Natal, 12 June 1939; d 16 November 2006

19 NOVEMBER 2011
BASIL D'OLIVEIRA
An Extraordinary Life
Scyld Berry

No professional cricketer can have had a career so full of emotion and controversy as Basil D'Oliveira. From his introduction as the first non-white South African in English county cricket, to his role in the banning of South Africa from international cricket and sport in general, to his long sad decline with Parkinson's disease, D'Oliveira's life was perhaps the most extraordinary the game has seen.

As a cricketer, he was a very good, powerfully built batsman and a competent bowler. He could have become a great batsman if the opportunity had come earlier in his career. He would never reveal his actual date of birth – he would not have been selected for Middleton, Worcestershire or England if he had – but he let it be known that he was born at least three years earlier than the 1931 date which he officially gave. In other words he was at least thirty-two when he was given a chance in league cricket, thirty-four when he qualified for Worcestershire, and thirty-eight when he was first chosen for England – and probably three to five years older. Thus his aggregates of 18,882 first-class runs at an average of 39.67 would surely have been more than doubled if he had been granted a normal career in a normal society. D'Oliveira, however, was unlucky enough to have been born a non-white in apartheid South Africa and brought up under the weight of all the discriminations that that system imposed. He was a Cape Coloured, though in 1995 when – for the first time since emigrating – he returned to the house where he grew up on Signal Hill in Cape Town during a visit funded by the *Sunday Telegraph*, he told me his forebears probably came from Madeira, not Malaya or Indonesia like most of his community: hence the Portuguese surname. Thus classified, what chance of a decent life did he have? Or, as John Arlott phrased it: 'What opportunity was there for a boy cricketer, denied by the laws of his native country organised coaching; parental financial capacity to afford proper gear; the use of a grass wicket or a safe outfield; the opportunity to take part in a first-class match or to play against opponents experienced at such a level?'

In non-white South African cricket, on rough pitches usually of matting, D'Oliveira hit eighty centuries before trying for better luck abroad: had he spent the first fifteen years of his adulthood in English first-class cricket he could have scored a similar number of first-class hundreds, in addition to the forty-three he actually made. His early experiences made him a back-foot player – the bounce being so unpredictable on semi-derelict grounds – with a short back-lift. A strict cricket-playing father, who monitored his performances without praise, combined with D'Oliveira's natural determination to succeed at what he did best.

In South Africa, the closest he came to 'official' cricket was when he sat in the cheap stands where non-whites were segregated at Newlands in Cape Town. He had given up hope of playing at such a level, was about to give up the game itself, and had just got married to Naomi from his own community, when the break came: for several years John Arlott, famous radio commentator and cricket correspondent of the *Guardian*, had been trying to persuade a league club in England to employ D'Oliveira as a professional. Naturally, none would – there was no evidence that Cape Coloureds could play organised cricket as they had never been given the chance – until Middleton in the Central Lancashire League had their pro cry off at the start of the 1960 season, needed a late replacement, and were persuaded to give D'Oliveira a go. Even then the club weren't prepared to risk much money, and his friends had to raise funds through charity matches in Cape Town so that he could make ends meet in a completely alien world. In his first weeks in England, on damp turf pitches, D'Oliveira could hardly make a run: twenty-five in his first five league innings.

The alien-ness was not confined to the cricket field. Brought up as a third-class citizen at best, the self-esteem beaten out of him by the South African system, he was not used to being treated as a human being. He was aghast, on the train journey north from London, at being allowed to sit in a restaurant car with white people; he was amazed at the sight of a television. He was far too insecure and shy to socialise and talk about cricket and the new techniques he had to learn in order to play swing and seam bowling. But the talent came out: he started to make runs, in stacks, until he topped the Central Lancashire League batting averages for the season ahead of the greatest all-round cricketer ever known, Garfield Sobers.

In 1964, obviously too good for league cricket, he qualified for Worcestershire – at the persuasion of his friend and teammate Tom Graveney – and helped them to retain the county championship the following year. Simply to make a place for himself in such a strong side, he had to become a reliable slip fielder and a good fourth seamer, as well as a dependable number five or six. He was certainly that: he made a century on his championship debut and another in his second championship match. As he had by now taken out a British passport, so that he could go on cricket tours to Asia without being turned away as a South African citizen, it was soon apparent that he would be good enough for England. And thus, as one of the oldest Test debutants, he walked out at Lord's in 1966 to a tremendous ovation – though he remarked later in his autobiography, *Time to Declare*, that he thought Headingley was the only English Test ground where the crowd was one hundred per cent behind him.

He was soon to be proved right about Lord's not being completely supportive. Even though he became an England regular, and scored a brilliant 158 against Australia at the Oval in 1968, the England selectors did not select him in the 16-man touring party to South Africa that winter. Pressures came from above, no doubt from the very top of government. D'Oliveira became the *cause célèbre*: a few voices at the top spoke up for him – Mike Brearley and David Sheppard most notably – but otherwise the cricket establishment was far keener on preserving traditional ties with apartheid South Africa than on striking a blow against institutionalised injustice. 'Sport and politics don't mix' was their slogan. Then Tom Cartwright pulled out of the original touring party through injury, D'Oliveira was selected in his place, and the South African prime minister John Vorster immediately called off the tour, affronted by the presence of a non-white in the England team.

As the controversy over sporting links with apartheid South Africa raged D'Oliveira maintained his outward calm and dignity, but he was not unscathed. The frustration ran deep, naturally. He revealed it in an anecdote in his autobiography, about a game in Scarborough in 1966 when he batted against the white South African fast bowler Peter Pollock: 'Now Pollock was a very aggressive quickie, a typical South African in fact. Well, he bowled me a beamer [a head-high full toss, now illegal] in this game at Scarborough and the crowd all went mad. I wasn't too keen either.

I was prepared to give him the benefit of the doubt, to think that the ball had slipped or that his footholds were troubling him – but no, he just looked straight at me grimly, didn't apologise or look at his footholds. All the anger and frustration of a coloured South African facing up to a white South African welled up inside me and I thought, "I'll get you". I didn't believe he would bowl another beamer at me so I decided to hit him out of sight next ball. Fortunately the ball pitched in just the right spot and I can still see it flying into the top of the stand and the crowd cheering themselves hoarse . . .' D'Oliveira and Pollock made up when they toured Australia together and the latter recognised the former as a fellow cricketer and human being.

In the rest of his on-field career Dolly – as he came to be known – helped England under Ray Illingworth to regain the Ashes in Australia in 1970–71, and to retain them by sharing the 1972 series, his last. By then he was at least forty-four, perhaps much older. In his forty-four Tests he also took forty-seven wickets at an average of 39, so that he bore the mark of an all-rounder in that his batting average was higher than his bowling. He developed something of a golden arm as a partnership-breaker with medium-paced outswing or off-spin. As a fielder it was perhaps fortunate that he did not play in the era of one-day internationals. Indeed, so leisurely was the pace of Test cricket that for his first two seasons with England he managed to play when unable to throw because of a shoulder injury.

Even in his restricted career, when he was past his physical prime, D'Oliveira was a formidably strong cricketer. But it was for the struggle which he experienced, and personified, and won, that he was famous and loved. He wondered why the English public for the most part took him to their hearts: perhaps because they like an underdog, he thought, 'in the way only the English can'. More than that though, as D'Oliveira walked out for his Test debut at Lord's, he symbolised a triumph of the human spirit in the face of injustice, cruelty, inhumanity. History may well decide that the lives of millions of non-white South Africans would have been made wretched for even longer but for Basil D'Oliveira.

Basil Lewis D'Oliveira: b Signal Hill, Cape Town, 4 October 1931; d 19 November 2011

15 DECEMBER 1991

JOHN ARLOTT
His Words Took Cricket Beyond the Boundary Rope

Tony Lewis

John Arlott ended his career as a radio cricket commentator in 1980 with the words: 'And after Trevor Bailey, it will be Christopher Martin-Jenkins.' He then left the Lord's commentary box, mopping his brow with the well-known red handkerchief, complaining, as he so often did, about the heat. He had been given a standing ovation by the Test crowd and even the cricketers of Australia and England stopped playing so they could turn and applaud, and pay tribute to the man whose golden voice had floated so deliciously, informatively and lovingly from that very pavilion top to all parts of the world.

I was one of his BBC colleagues that day and, after he had padded down the steps from the back of the box, I said: 'I thought you would have said more at the end, remembered more. I thought you would be more romantic.' He gave me the familiar loving scowl: 'What's more romantic than the clean break?' A message came later, which was an invitation to have lunch with the M.C.C. Never an Establishment man, he turned it down. 'Why now? They never asked me before. In any case, never much liked Lord's.'

Arlott began his memorable career as a clerk in a mental hospital followed by eleven years with Southampton Borough Police, where he became a detective sergeant. He joined the BBC in 1945 and, for a time, was a poetry producer, working with Dylan Thomas. By 1946 he had begun cricket commentaries, and by the summer of 1947 was covering the game continuously. The following year, his commentaries on Bradman's all-conquering Australians brought accolades, and huge audiences, on the BBC Light Programme. For the next thirty-two years, his voice became synonymous with the English summer Tests.

Arlott was always his own man. He enjoyed language, found cricket fascinating as a true mirror of life but, above all, he loved cricketers. It was by placing himself inside the cricketer's head that he could hear the heart beat, understand the hopes, the fears, the financial frailty of the job, the worries and the hard-learnt skills. He always said of his Hampshire men that he could understand a Leo Harrison as well as a Barry Richards, and somehow better because successes came with greater difficulty to Leo.

The cricketers he described came to life because he set them in the broader weave of life, and he elevated the game because of that. For him, this was not a game played remotely inside boundaries. His own world was wide. A collector of fine glass, aquatints, furniture and first editions, he was also a wine connoisseur and wrote on the subject for the *Guardian*. In addition, he tried to enter Parliament, unsuccessfully contesting Epping for the Liberals in 1955 and 1959. When I was a player with Glamorgan I used to gather Sunderland lustre and Stevengraphs for his collection, while he picked up small pieces of Georgian silver for mine. Over a glass of wine in some pub on the circuit we would make our exchanges.

His commentaries stood out above those of the mere talkers because he had the clear mind of the poet, reducing emotions to a word and passages of play to a sentence. 'Kapil Dev beats Butcher's outside edge,' he intoned in 1979. 'Butcher hangs his head, holds his bat behind his back in both hands ... now looks up the pitch at Kapil Dev like a small boy caught stealing jam.'

Because he was a man of sympathies, he had his hates as well. He detested South Africa and refused to broadcast their tours. He had no time for falseness and was bitter that he lost a son in a needless road accident. He constantly wore a black tie.

I last visited Arlott in Alderney, where he had retreated, on his seventieth birthday. He met me in the one small airport room, heaved the familiar leather briefcase on to the counter alongside the receptionist and took out a couple of glasses, a corkscrew and a bottle of Beaune. 'It's been too long,' he said. He had chosen Alderney because the island had given him so much pleasure at a particular time of his life. He never gave the impression of following cricket closely from that distance, but still wrote prolifically and professionally.

These are just a few of the million recollections which will pour out from a multitude of people as he leaves us. What wonderful pleasure his talents gave us. How cricket is in his debt.

**Leslie Thomas John Arlott: b Basingstoke,
25 February. 1914; d 14 December, 1991**

6 JANUARY 1994
BRIAN JOHNSTON
A Gentleman Among Players

There can scarcely be anyone in Britain who does not feel bereaved by the death of Brian Johnston. Though he was most celebrated for his unique role as the heart and soul of the BBC's *Test Match Special*, it is not only followers of cricket who will miss him. As presenter of *Down Your Way*, and as one of the BBC's most prolific broadcasters on both radio and television since the War, Mr Johnston was a regular and welcome visitor to our homes for nearly half a century. He was a landmark of English culture. In his charm, articulacy, good manners and, above all, his great good humour, he embodied all that was best about the golden age of broadcasting. His was a personality and an approach that are, today, all too rare in the increasingly charmless world of what we can now call 'the media'. Nor was Mr Johnston's persona merely one manufactured for the microphone. He was the genuine article, as his many friends, and the many good causes for whom he raised money, will readily testify.

But it is cricket for which we shall best remember him. Just as one favoured either Hutton or Compton, or Gower or Gooch, so in the commentary box the choice was between Arlott and Johnston. Arlott had all the poetry, the languid, melancholy reflectiveness of a man oppressively aware of his own mortality. Johnners, though, was one for whom every day was like the first morning of a Lord's

Test: high summer, brilliant sunshine, England batting and going well. He was that kind of Englishman, once so common, now so rare, who had the Dunkirk Spirit flowing through his veins, and whose mission was to take the lead in cheering us all up. No English collapse could be so dire, no break for rain so long, that Johnners, cake in hand, was ever stuck for the means of entertaining us. A professional to his marrow, he radiated the assurance and *joie de vivre* of the highly gifted amateur. He carried his love of cricket, and the wider applications of that sporting ethos, through life like, as Newbolt would have put it, a torch in flame.

Brian Alexander Johnston: b Little Berkhamsted, 24 June, 1912; d 5 January, 1994

30 JANUARY 2009
BILL FRINDALL
The Scorer with an Obsessive Eye
for Detail

Bill Frindall was from 1966 the scorer for *Test Match Special* on BBC Radio, nicknamed 'The Bearded Wonder' for his lustrous facial hair and encyclopaedic knowledge of cricket facts. A schoolmaster introduced Frindall to cricket scoring one rainy sports afternoon when he was a boy, and he went on to become the longest-serving member of the *Test Match Special* team, covering more than three hundred and fifty Test matches, which he considered the only 'proper' form of the game. Frindall took over the scoring for *Test Match Special* in June 1966, following the death of the previous incumbent, Arthur Wrigley, who had been the BBC scorer since 1934. On joining he soon developed a strong relationship with the commentator John Arlott, who is reported to have said to him: 'I hear you like driving – that's good, because I like drinking. I think we're going to get on.'

Frindall was known for the fabulous complexity of his scoring charts, a modified version of the linear system developed by the Australian Bill Ferguson. Safely hidden behind a Thermos in the corner of the commentary box, he applied a host of coded symbols to three separate scoring sheets, noting shots played or attempted, and the response of the fielding side. It is now known as

'Frindallgram' and often required the rapid input of a huge amount of detail, especially after the fall of a wicket. 'The secret is to keep calm,' he said. He was later dubbed the 'taciturn rock around which commentary ebbs and flows'. Indeed, his calculations were so invariably accurate that if Frindall's tally diverged from the one on the scoreboard, the commentators would not hesitate in following his version.

His astonishing ability to recall the most obscure and arcane snippets of cricket trivia was as much a part of the *Test Match Special* experience as the runs, wickets and discussions about cake. 'Johnners,' Frindall noted about his *TMS* colleague Brian Johnston, who came up with the 'Bearders' nickname, 'delighted in asking the most impossible questions.' His eye for detail could border on the obsessive however, and he refused to recognise an I.C.C.-sponsored Test match between Australia and the Rest of the World in 2005. As such, when Shane Warne took what the rest of the cricketing community agreed was his seven hundredth wicket the following year, Frindall insisted it was really his six hundred and ninety-fourth.

He was present at several episodes which have gone down in *TMS* lore, including the moment that Jonathan Agnew prompted corpsing in the box by suggesting that Ian Botham, who had trodden on his stumps, had 'failed to get his leg over'. 'The initial silence,' noted Agnew, 'was followed by a clatter of china' as an aghast Frindall dropped his teacup. Other japes included Frindall turning up to score one day of an Ashes Test in fancy dress. 'I remember Bill turning up one day at the Oval wearing a full Arab costume complete with headdress and sunglasses,' said the former *TMS* producer Peter Baxter. 'It came as quite a surprise to the commentators. When he arrived at the ground, the steward told him, "You can't park there – that's Bill Frindall's spot". He replied, "Too bad – I've bought the Oval".' Not considered the easiest man to get along with in the cricketing world, however, Frindall was not always included in such fun and games, or welcomed as a natural part of a relaxed evening out on tour.

He was an enthusiastic cricketer in his youth, and his 'fast' bowling prowess was on display at cricket grounds in charity matches for many years. Friends noted, however, that he 'couldn't bat, and ran faster than he bowled'. His own touring team, known as the Malta Maniacs, had their own tie with a Maltese Cross on it. Among those who once played for them was the Duchess of York's father, Major Ronald Ferguson.

**William Howard Frindall: b Epsom,
3 March, 1939; d 29 January, 2009**

I MARCH 1990
COLIN MILBURN
Cavalier Batsman Beloved
by Everyone

Tony Lewis

Colin Milburn first caught the attention of the cricket world when he scored a century before lunch for his native Durham against the Indian tourists in 1959. In the early 1960s, when he began his professional career, Milburn's batting gave a vivid splash of colour to county cricket. Certainly, there had never been a player like him before in Northampton – cavalier, with a range of both brutal and beautiful strokes. Much of his batting was from the textbook, orthodox in defence, neat off his legs, but his square-driving on the off side and his thumping hooks and pulls were all his own. He was a steady medium-fast bowler and an agile short-leg fielder – despite his eighteen stone.

Many doubted his ability to repeat his county form in Tests, but he was in terrific form in 1966, hitting three hundreds before lunch. He continued in a spectacular way, but there was no game he devastated more than the one between Western Australia, for whom he was playing, and Queensland at Perth in 1969. He hit the Queensland attack for 243 by tea-time and was out first ball after the interval.

The tragic car crash, in which he lost an eye, happened in the early hours of the morning after a night out with his great friend, Hylton

Ackerman, at the Sywell Motel in Northamptonshire. Milburn loved parties and late nights. His re-entry to cricket circles, with an artificial eye and impaired sight in the remaining one, made him most depressed. When he tried television commentary at Lord's, I called into his room on the morning after to see how he was going. He just wept and said he had been able to see nothing in detail all day. Later, his sight improved and he made one last grasp at the game. In 1973, he played a few matches for Northamptonshire – but it was no good.

My last night out with him was during the Manchester Test last year. Our taxi driver refused to take a fare from him, and in the bar the first round was on the management. Everyone in the world was as pleased to greet Colin Milburn, because he embodied enviable good cheer and a highly individual passage through life.

Colin Milburn: b Burnopfield, County Durham, 23 October 1941; d 28 February 1990

27 APRIL 2007
ARTHUR MILTON
My Opening Partner was
a Joy to Bat With
David Green

I first met Arthur Milton in The Parks in 1959 when playing my first first-class match for Oxford University against Gloucestershire. Milton was an established county batsman and had made his Test debut the previous year, thus becoming an international at both cricket and football – the last man to do so. I scratched about against John Mortimore before being dismissed without scoring. On a pair, and again confronted by Morty's flighty off-spin, I got an inside edge and watched the ball go knee-high to Arthur, one of the game's great close catchers, at backward short leg. Arthur, to my astonished gratitude, parted his hands, letting the ball go through for three, his kindly gesture sparing a raw and nervous nineteen-year-old the ignominy of a pair on debut.

I got to know Arthur well in 1968 when, having been sacked by Lancashire, I joined Gloucestershire. My technique was in tatters and confidence very low. Arthur took me under his wing and, with Morty's help, rebuilt my game. Like most struggling batsmen I was moving too early, planting my front foot on middle and off. Arthur got me to delay my first movement, simply by suggesting an extra tap of the bat on the crease as the bowler released the ball. Another priceless lesson he taught me was to recognise the possibility of stolen singles from defensive strokes. Arthur saw runs where I would never have believed half a run existed. He persuaded me that if gully was right-handed, a ball rolling slowly to his left meant an easy single. One slight complication was in calling, for Arthur didn't call at all. If he wanted a run he would advance a couple of quick paces, raising an eyebrow inquiringly at the same time. I learnt to trust his judgment absolutely.

We opened the innings together a fair amount in my first year with Gloucestershire and he was immensely helpful, not just because of all the singles I was picking up through his influence. Playing against Worcestershire at Cheltenham on a pitch helping spin, I had just survived an over from England left-armer Norman Gifford. Arthur came down the pitch and said: 'Are you all right down there?' 'No, I'm not,' I answered. 'Well, I'll push for one next over and come down that end,' he replied. This he did, playing Gifford in complete comfort and enabling me to make a decent score rather than suffer an early dismissal.

Two opening partnerships that year I particularly remember. We put on 315 in just over four hours against Sussex at Hove, at the time a record for Gloucestershire in the championship. Then, against Nottinghamshire at Trent Bridge in a Gillette Cup quarter-final, we made 160 together, the stand ending with my dismissal ten minutes before lunch. I found him a joy to bat with. His calm, relaxed approach seemed to rub off on me. Arthur always played beautifully, sideways on and with a wide range of strokes. Of middle height and sparely built, he favoured the back foot, cutting deftly and deflecting with great certainty off his legs. He also drove in the arc between cover and wide mid-on, the certainty of his placements rather than power ensuring he got full value for his strokes.

**Clement Arthur Milton: b Bedminster, Bristol,
10 March 1928; d 25 April 2007**

23 MARCH 2011
FRED TITMUS
A True Master of His Craft
Scyld Berry

When Graeme Swann is acclaimed as England's best off-spin bowler since Jim Laker, it is another way of saying that Swann has edged past Fred Titmus. In terms of English cricket, praise does not come much higher. For Titmus was a master of his craft, and that did not include off-spin alone, though he took an astonishing 2,830 first-class wickets with it. He was also a master of neat, late-middle-order strokeplay, of such orthodoxy that when he toured Australia in 1974–75 at the advanced age of forty-two, he could still make 61 in the Perth Test. And open the batting in 1964 when England needed an emergency opener.

He was a master of the rest of his craft, too: the transmission of the folklore of Middlesex and England cricket to the next generation, whether as a player or a county coach or an England selector, whether over a cup of tea or a pint or a pipe. It was not a physically tough world, compared to what English professional cricket is now with its boot camps, fitness training and strength conditioning, but it was still a hard old school, which never erred on the side of encouraging the young. Titmus not only survived but mastered it – undaunted by the hierarchical distinctions exemplified by the public announcement at Lord's: 'For F.J. Titmus on your scorecard, please read Titmus F.J.'

He lost four toes in a boating accident on England's tour of the West Indies in 1967–68, but never his line and length. Swann snares his victims by turning his off-breaks, Titmus gained his by drifting past their outside edge, to be caught by John Murray behind the wicket or by Peter Parfitt at slip. Swann, from the start of his run-up, puts more into each delivery. Titmus took a couple of ambling shuffles up to the stumps and rocked back, but this economy of effort enabled him to play championship cricket in five separate decades, an achievement that will not be matched again.

Titmus averaged just less than three wickets in his fifty-three Tests. Swann has taken more than four wickets per Test. In a far more leisurely age, Titmus took a Test wicket every ninety-eight balls; Swann – so far – one every fifty-eight balls. In the spirit of those times, bowlers were allowed to bowl so long as they pitched a length. Nobody would run down the pitch and smash the ball straight back. Titmus was not slog-swept or reverse-swept. He conceded just less than two runs an over in Tests to Swann's just under three.

Into this orderly, hierarchical world Titmus appeared in 1949, when Middlesex were short and he had to make his debut at Bath. His apprenticeship was so thorough not only because he had to bowl for hours in the nets at Lord's but because, on National Service, he could play for the Combined Services against the first-class counties and get mistakes out of his system. Like one of his non-turning off-breaks, Titmus drifted past his opponents during the 1950s and into the England side. To become Laker's successor he had to surpass other master-craftsmen: David Allen and John Mortimore of Gloucestershire, Ray Illingworth and Don Shepherd.

Playing thirty-odd first-class games a season, he did the double of one thousand runs and one hundred wickets eight times – the same as Trevor Bailey. He scored 21,588 first-class runs in addition to his

2,830 wickets – figures which Swann will match if he keeps going at his current rate for forty more years. The last of his wickets came in late 1982 when Mike Brearley saw the pipe smoke in Middlesex's dressing room and decided he needed a third spinner. So different is cricket now that it is worth asking if an off-spinner could amble to the stumps and survive in this age of powerful batsmen with their mighty willows, their slog-sweeps and reverse-sweeps – or whether Titmus would be taken to the cleaners every time. And there was an answer of sorts in Dhaka on Wednesday, when Pakistan opened their bowling with an off-spinner who took no more than two or three shuffles, and who turned hardly a ball, but who landed every one in the 'right areas' as they say now. Mohammad Hafeez went on to be man of the match.

Frederick John Titmus: b Kentish Town, London, 24 November 1932; d 23 March 2011

2 OCTOBER 2012

DON WILSON

The Asthmatic Who Relished
the Outdoor Life

Don Wilson bowled slow left-arm in the great Yorkshire side who won seven county championships between 1959 and 1968; having played six Tests for England he went on to become an immensely popular M.C.C. head coach at Lord's. As a boy he suffered from chronic asthma, so his father, an ambulance man, saved up to take him for a consultation in Harley Street where, only seven years old, Don told the doctor he wanted to be a cricketer. 'That's the perfect job for you,' came the reply. 'Out in the fresh air.' The course of his life was altered when, in a Sunday benefit match at Settle, he bowled the great Len Hutton. This led to an invitation to attend nets at Headingley, where his first session with the bat, facing the full pace of Fred Trueman, did not impress the coach Arthur Mitchell: 'What do you do for a living, lad? Well, forget the cricket. Fetch some bloody timber and board that end up.'

Wilson made his championship debut, aged nineteen, filling in for Johnny Wardle, who was playing for England. The role of slow left-arm bowler – from Bobby Peel, Wilfred Rhodes, Hedley Verity through to Wardle – had always been crucial to Yorkshire's success. The next year, Wardle fell out with the newly appointed captain, the amateur Ronnie Burnet, and was sacked in midseason. Suddenly the inexperienced Wilson had to maintain the great tradition, playing in front of Yorkshire crowds angry at the loss of one of their stars. He was not a great spinner of the ball, relying more on subtle changes of flight and pace, but, with the canny off-spinner Ray Illingworth at the other end, he was soon winning over the sceptics. Burnet brought in several players he had captained in the second team, and a new youthful spirit brought the championship title back to Yorkshire in 1959, after ten painful years without success.

Wilson took one hundred wickets in a season five times in the 1960s. 'Wils had an easy run-up, a nice delivery stride and a high action,' his team-mate Ken Taylor recalled. 'And he was so enthusiastic. He expected a wicket every ball, throwing his arms up and widening his eyes. Even if the ball didn't penetrate the batsman, his eyes did.' He was also an outstanding fielder at mid-wicket, and as a lusty lower-order hitter contributed useful runs, none more spectacular than his innings at Worcester in 1961 when, against all advice, he went out to bat with his left arm in plaster. With nine wickets down and thirty-six runs still wanted, his intention was to block out the last few minutes for the draw – but, true to the title of his autobiography, *Mad Jack*, he got carried away by the occasion. Holding the bat with only his top hand, he flailed six fours, three of them in an over off the fearsome Jack Flavell – who was bowling at high speed with a new ball. Then he hit Len Coldwell, another England bowler, back over his head and strode off victorious with 29 not out.

He toured India in 1963–64, playing all five Tests and also toured Australia with Illingworth's Ashes-winning party of 1970–71. However, in his latter years at Yorkshire he developed the yips, unable to run up and pitch the ball. He retired at the end of 1974, after which he had three happy years captaining Lincolnshire.

It was a great shock to him, however, when he received a telephone call from E.W. Swanton, cricket correspondent for the *Daily Telegraph*, asking him if he would like to become M.C.C.'s head coach. It was a most unlikely appointment. 'You're not mixing me up with the Wilson who played for Kent, are you?' he was tempted to ask Swanton.

In the event the choice proved inspired. Wilson enjoyed working with the Test players when they called at Lord's for help; and, perhaps even more, he loved the days when he spread the joys of cricket to wide-eyed schoolchildren. Peter O'Toole became a friend, calling regularly for a net, and on one famous occasion he was the only batsman available when Imran Khan arrived, wanting to bowl at full pace ahead of the World Cup in Australia. 'Peter was bruised from head to foot,' Wilson said, 'but he loved it. It was like he was Lawrence of Arabia all over again.'

Donald Wilson: b Settle, 7 August 1937; d 21 July 2012

28 AUGUST 2007
ROY McLEAN
A Fearsome Proposition
When in the Groove

Roy McLean was an aggressive middle-order right-hand batsman for South Africa, representing his country in forty Test matches in the 1950s and 1960s. A fluent and powerful strokemaker, when he was on song McLean could be a fearsome proposition, particularly square of the wicket. Early in his career he showed a tendency towards recklessness, and he remained inconsistent (in Tests he was dismissed without scoring on eleven occasions); but he matured with the years, and once moved Donald Bradman to observe: 'When Roy plays a good innings, no one can hold him. He can score off any type of bowling.'

McLean's most famous contribution in a Test match came on the tour to Australia in 1952–53. It was assumed that the Australians – then fielding players of the calibre of Neil Harvey, Ray Lindwall and Keith Miller – merely had to turn up to win the series, and when the final Test began at Melbourne the home side were 2–1 up; they duly accumulated 520 in their first innings, Harvey's contribution being 205. The South Africans, however, replied with 435, John Watkins scoring 92 and McLean 81. The Australians were then dismissed for 209, leaving the tourists needing 295 to win and square the series. McLean came in when his team were 191 for four, and as he left the pavilion to make his way to the crease his anxious captain, Jack Cheetham, cautioned him against giving away his wicket. 'Don't worry, Pop, I'll get them for you,' McLean replied. Having been dropped off his first ball, he hit an unbeaten 76, seeing the South Africans home with six wickets to spare. McLean's Test average on the tour was 41.11.

McLean also played rugby for Natal, and in 1953, after frustrating the Australians with his cricket bat at Melbourne, he now embarrassed them as a fly-half: a strong Wallabies team were leading Natal with just seconds remaining when McLean received the ball from scrum-half Tich Taylor and scored a drop goal for his side to win the match 15–14.

**Roy Alastair McLean: b Pietermaritzburg, Natal,
9 July 1930; d 26 August 2007**

9 AUGUST 2003
RUSSELL ENDEAN
South African Who Took One of
the Most Amazing Catches

Russell Endean played an important role in stiffening South Africa's batting during the early 1950s; he was also one of the most brilliant fielders in the history of the game. The onus of propping up his country's unreliable batting made him a somewhat dour batsman at the highest level, and won him the sobriquet 'Endless Endean'. Certainly in Tests he was more remarkable for his will-power and concentration than for his strokeplay. Formidably sound in defence, he gathered his runs rather by deflections behind the wicket than by the dashing strokeplay exemplified by his friend and team-mate Roy McLean.

Endean, though, could claim credit for two memorable South African victories, against Australia at Melbourne in December 1952, and against England at Headingley in July 1955. He reached his zenith in Australia in 1952–53. Before arriving, the South African side, captained by Jack Cheetham, had been considered so weak that there had even been talk of cancelling the tour. How could the young and inexperienced Springboks possibly match an Australian team containing such players as Arthur Morris, Neil Harvey, Lindsay Hassett, Keith Miller, Richie Benaud, Ray Lindwall and Bill Johnston? In the event, the South Africans' inspired team spirit

– manifested especially in their magnificent fielding, the best seen up to that time – enabled them to square the series at two-all, with one match drawn.

Another key factor was the unexpected success of Endean, who topped South Africa's Test averages with 438 runs at an average of 48.66. His greatest moment came in the second Test at Melbourne, when he batted for seven hours in the second innings to make a chanceless 162 not out and set up South Africa's victory by eighty-two runs. In that same match Endean took one of the most amazing catches ever seen, when, standing with his back against the iron boundary fence at long on, he leapt high and clung one-handed on to a rasping drive from Keith Miller. 'I didn't realise Russell had caught it until I heard Keith Miller go off pop,' remembered John Waite, South Africa's wicketkeeper. 'What he said is unprintable.' The Melbourne crowd also had to overcome its astonishment before cheering the fielder for a full minute. Endean was equally brilliant at snapping up chances close to the wicket. He took twenty-nine catches on the tour; when he finally missed a chance in the fourth Test at Adelaide, the crowd was stunned into silence.

Endean was involved in two unusual Test dismissals. At the Oval in 1951, a ball from the off-spinner Athol Rowan lifted sharply and struck Len Hutton on the glove. It ran up his arm, and seemed to him to be falling on to his wicket. Instinctively, Hutton flicked at it with his bat, without thinking that he was preventing Endean, the wicketkeeper, from making a catch. When the South Africans appealed he was given out for 'obstructing the field'. Batting against England at Newlands, Cape Town, in 1957, Endean himself was given out 'handled the ball'. After he had padded away a delivery from Jim Laker, the ball spun up towards the stumps, and he illegally used his hand to keep it out.

His most remarkable – and most uncharacteristic – innings was the 235 he made against Orange Free State in December 1954, when he established a world record by making 197 not out before lunch. He would probably have reached his double century before the interval but for the frustration of having to watch his partner play out the last over.

**William Russell Endean: Johannesburg, Transvaal,
b 31 May 1924; d 28 June 2003**

31 DECEMBER 2005
EDDIE BARLOW
A Cricketer Fizzing with Aggression
and Determination

Eddie Barlow was a fine all-round cricketer, and a key member of the great South Africa side of the late 1960s. As a boy Barlow was far from looking like a sporting hero. His spectacles and stout build earned him the nickname 'Bunter'; indeed, he was so short-sighted that (so the story went) he could hardly see over the front wheel of his bicycle when he rode to school. As he grew, however, the podginess turned to muscle, so that 'tough' and 'burly' became more appropriate descriptions than 'unathletic' and 'fat'. His strength helped to make him a formidable opening batsman.

Sound in defence, he loved to force the ball through the field off the back foot. He also developed into a more than useful medium-pace bowler, capable of swinging the ball sharply. And very little escaped his fast reactions at slip. Something of Bunter remained, however, in his untidiness. Charles Fortune once described him as running up to bowl 'looking like an unmade bed'. Again, though, appearances were deceptive. For Barlow, so modest and easy-going in private life, was a highly combative cricketer on the field, fizzing with aggression and determination.

He reserved his best performances for Tests against Australia. In his first innings against them, at Brisbane in December 1963, he made a century, and then followed up with another in the next Test at Melbourne. Then at Adelaide, in the fourth Test, he scored 201, sharing in a stand of 341 in 283 minutes with Graeme Pollock. They guided South Africa to a thumping ten-wicket victory which gave early warning of the side's potential. Barlow also scored heavily against Mike Smith's England side in South Africa in 1964–65, including 138 and 78 at Cape Town, and 96 at Johannesburg. At Cape Town, however, he incurred the wrath of the England players by failing to walk when apparently caught in the gully off Fred Titmus. Bowler and batsman exchanged heated comments, and the atmosphere remained tense for the rest of the day. No England player applauded when Barlow reached his century; by contrast Tony Pithey was ostentatiously congratulated when he reached his fifty.

In 1969–70, in South Africa, Ali Bacher's magnificent team again trounced Australia, this time by 4–0 in four Test matches. Barlow contributed two more centuries, before the banning of South Africa over the apartheid issue ended his Test career. This was particularly hard on Barlow, who always took a liberal and progressive view in matters of race. Later in 1970 he turned out for the Rest of the World against England. At Headingley he performed the hat-trick, which he immediately extended to four wickets in five balls.

From 1976 to 1978 Barlow was co-opted by Derbyshire, for whom his enthusiasm proved as valuable as his excellent personal performances. Taking over the captaincy halfway through 1976, he insisted on high standards of fitness, and succeeded in dragging the county up to seventh place in the championship in 1977. He also took them to a final at Lord's.

**Edgar John Barlow: b Pretoria, Transvaal,
12 August 1940; d 30 December 2005**

30 DECEMBER 2012
TONY GREIG
The Hand That Rocked
Cricket's Cradle

Tony Greig was born a South African but became captain of England. His very considerable achievements as an all-rounder, however, were largely forgotten after he decided in 1977 to defy the cricketing establishment by helping the Australian media tycoon Kerry Packer to launch World Series Cricket. Overnight, the glamour boy of English cricket was transformed by press and officialdom into an arch-betrayer. Yet so much about Greig was admirable: on the pitch he possessed the panache and the courage to match his ultra-competitive spirit; off it, he was unfailingly good-humoured and friendly.

Standing six feet six inches tall, fair-haired and handsome, Greig seemed created to stand out from the crowd. His greatest asset, though, was a temperament that relished confrontation and thrived on the big occasion. Thus his record as a batsman was far superior within the Test arena than outside it. In 350 first-class matches he scored 16,660 runs (including twenty-six centuries) at an average of 31.19. In fifty-eight Tests, by contrast, he made 3,599 runs (including eight centuries) and averaged 40.43. His first instinct was to attack. In batting, this often meant using his height to reach out and thrash the ball. He was talented enough, however, to match his play to the situation, as he showed in his greatest

Test innings, the 110 he scored at Brisbane in 1974 against Lillee and Thomson in their prime. His fellow England players had been less than delighted by his penchant for aggravating these ferocious bowlers by peppering them with bouncers. Greig himself, though, remained entirely unfazed. At Brisbane he deliberately cut over the slips, then added insult to injury by signalling his own fours. And when the bowlers tried a fuller length, they would be magnificently driven to the boundary.

As a bowler Greig defied expectation. Given his height and athleticism, it might have been imagined that he would hurl down thunderbolts. His approach to the crease, however, was curiously laboured and awkward, leaving him to rely on swing, bounce and cut rather than extreme pace. He also developed an alternative bowling style, sending down quickish off-breaks which at first seemed to carry little threat. Suddenly, though, against the West Indies at Port-of-Spain in 1974, he became deadly in this style, returning match figures of thirteen for 156 to enable England to square the series. Greig never again recorded such sensational figures. Nevertheless, for the next three years, after Garry Sobers retired from Test cricket, he was the most successful all-rounder in the world. He would end his Test career with 141 wickets at 32.20 apiece, and his first-class career with 856 victims at 28.85 each. A brilliant fielder, he also proved adept at exerting pressure by standing alarmingly close to batsmen.

Greig had made his first-class debut for Sussex in 1967, and in 1973 took over the captaincy. Full of zest, energy and enthusiasm, though never shy in berating error, he won the affection of both members and players. That summer he led the county to the final of the Gillette Cup, though they lost to Gloucestershire at Lord's. Ultimately, though, his record as county captain was disappointing, due in some part to his frequent absence on Test duty.

As captain of England for fourteen Tests from 1975 to 1977, Greig took over the reins when the team were at a low ebb, and inspired some recovery. It was no disgrace to lose against the all-powerful West Indies in 1976. Greig, however, received some well-deserved stick because he had predicted that he would make the tourists 'grovel'. He showed himself far more canny in India in 1976–77, when he began the tour by announcing that he had the greatest faith in Indian umpires. England won the series by three Tests to one. And if the Centenary Test against Australia in March 1977 was lost by forty-five runs – exactly the same margin as in the first Test in 1877 – there were universal plaudits for a splendid match.

At this point, however, with his career at its zenith, Greig entered into negotiations with Kerry Packer to defy M.C.C. and the Australian board in setting up World Series Cricket, which would operate outside the traditional structures of the game. He himself became Packer's chief publicist and set about recruiting the best players in the world. Sacked in consequence from the captaincy of England, Greig still played under Mike Brearley in the official home series against Australia in 1977, which England won – validation of the team's improvement under Greig's leadership. He also made some valuable runs, notably innings of 91 at Lord's and 76 at Old Trafford. To the traditionalists, however, he had become a pariah. John Woodcock, cricket correspondent of *The Times*, explained Greig's behaviour by pointing out that 'he was not English through and through'. Yet Greig had certainly done the state some service. He was, moreover, admirably unhypocritical about his motives in throwing in his lot with Packer: 'I did it for Tony Greig first, and for my family. Secondly, I did it because the Establishment deserved it.' There was something in that, given that cricketers had been so abysmally paid up to 1977. No one could plausibly maintain that the Packer experiment, which ended in 1979, ruined the game.

Indeed, in the long run it strikingly improved the lot of professional cricketers.

However, his association with Packer not only cast him in the role of Judas, it also damaged his prowess as a cricketer. Though appointed captain of the World XI, he suddenly seemed unequal to the challenge on the field. This may have been because his energies were taken up by his work as Packer's factotum. For whatever reason, his performances were so poor that he felt bound to drop himself from the second World Series.

Back in England, the renegade was dismissed from the Sussex captaincy at the beginning of 1978. Though he played a few more games for the county, it was now clear both that his cricket career was over and that his future lay in Australia. Kerry Packer remained supportive, making Greig managing director of Lion Insurance brokers in Sydney, and installing him as a commentator on Channel Nine. Greig proved a success before the microphone, especially enjoying his banter with Bill Lawry and his old rival Ian Chappell. His voice was heard in Britain once more when Sky employed him in 1990 to comment on England's Test series in the West Indies. He also worked for Channel 4 during the thrilling Ashes series of 2005.

A serious challenge to Greig's sporting ambitions had become evident at fourteen when he suffered an epileptic fit. He learnt the importance of getting sufficient sleep, even developing the capacity to nod off while waiting to bat. Though he remained liable to the occasional fit, his malady was generally kept secret, even from his fellow cricketers.

Anthony William Greig: b Queenstown, Cape Province, 6 October, 1946; d 29 December, 2012

8 SEPTEMBER 2000
ROY FREDERICKS
Swashbuckling Batsman Who
Murdered Fast Bowling

Roy Fredericks was an opening batsman of remarkable dash and flair, even by West Indian standards. A short man, not more than five foot six (*Wisden* put him at a mere five foot four), his chief aim in life was to murder fast bowling, if possible from the very first ball of the innings. Colin Croft, one of the most terrifying bowlers of all time, admitted that when he bowled at Fredericks, it was the fielders at gully and point who were scared, so fiercely did the left-handed 'Freddo' clout the ball. But Fredericks's defining shot was the hook. Earlier in 2000 he reflected that recent West Indian batsmen had become less inclined to play that shot, partly because of the deterioration of pitches in the Caribbean, partly because they lacked the necessary instinct. 'That is in you, to hook,' he believed. 'You can't tell nobody to hook. It's about confidence.'

No one had more confidence and courage than Fredericks, and his swashbuckling approach produced one of the great Test innings. In December 1975, the West Indies arrived in Perth for the second Test match against the Australians under heavy criticism for their irresponsible approach to batting in the first Test. Fredericks's response, on a lightning-fast wicket, was to hook Dennis Lillee's second ball for six, albeit off the top edge. The West Indies went into bat ninety minutes before lunch. At the interval, after fourteen overs, Fredericks was 81 not out, and the West Indies' score 130. His century came in 118 minutes off only seventy-three balls. Lillee and Thomson, two great fast bowlers then at their peak, were helpless as Fredericks raced on to 169 out of 258 in 217 minutes. He had faced 145 balls. It was a moment of imperishable glory.

Of course, the hook shot sometimes got Fredericks out. In the World Cup final of 1975, he immediately lofted Lillee into the crowd, only to slip and dislodge a bail. (He had not bothered with studs on his boots.) Against England in 1976, he was twice caught at long leg for nought, giving ample fodder to his critics. But Fredericks still averaged 57.44 in that series, scoring 138 in the second innings at Lord's, and another century at Headingley. In the second innings at the Oval, he and Gordon Greenidge put England to the sword, allowing the West Indies to declare after one hundred and forty minutes, with the total at 180 for no wicket.

The remarkable thing about Fredericks, considering the way he played, was his consistency. From the start of his international career in 1968–69 against Australia to his last Test, against Pakistan in 1977, he hardly had a bad series, though he looked vulnerable against spin early in his career. He could even, if the mood took him, play at responsibility. His 150 against England at Edgbaston in 1973 took eight and a half hours, one of the most tedious displays seen from a West Indian batsman. Happily, such restraint was rare. More often, the jaunty tilt of his cap at the crease proclaimed a cricketer who believed that the manner in which the game was played counted for more than grinding out a victory.

Roy Clifton Fredericks: b Blairmont, Berbice, Guyana, 11 November 1942; d 5 September 2000

25 MARCH 2007
BOB WOOLMER
The Outsider Accepted
Everywhere He Went
Scyld Berry

Bob Woolmer, who will be forever remembered for the way he died, deserves to be remembered for his cricket too. He batted as he coached and lived. There were no sharp edges, nothing spiky or confrontational, in his cover-driving or his speech. He was softly spoken, smooth and accomplished, an outsider who was accepted wherever he went because, for a passport, he had his lifelong enthusiasm for cricket.

He scored three Test centuries for England, coached the most successful county side of all time – Warwickshire in 1994 – and made South Africa second only to Australia. But he was at his best as a batting consultant for it was then, as when he was I.C.C.'s high performance manager, that his enthusiasm shone through. And in that lies irony, because by training up associate members like Ireland, he helped to bring about their defeat of Pakistan in the 2007 World Cup.

One day in Zimbabwe he took me to the Academy in Harare. The plan had been for us both to address a group of twenty or so boys, but once Woolmer had a bat in his hands, the words and strokes flowed. He was a 'like pole' with Duncan Fletcher: both of them coaches domiciled in Cape Town, both fascinated by the theories and practices of cricket and batting in particular. But Woolmer was as talkative in public as Fletcher is taciturn. He kept it simple as the best teachers do, limiting himself to a couple of main points, which is as much as the beginner's brain can absorb. By the time he had finished talking about the left elbow, and the importance of removing the front leg from the line of delivery when hitting to leg, it was not only the Academy boys who felt they could bat for their country.

On another occasion we met at one of those impossibly beautiful wineries in the Western Cape, in the hinterland of Cape Town, settled by the Dutch and as manicured as a model's fingernail. The second Test between 'his' South Africa and England had just been drawn, owing to the five-session rearguard innings of 185 not out by Mike Atherton. Woolmer acknowledged it was a fine innings, but he was a skilful propagandist, too. England, having been set 479 to win, had lost their first four wickets cheaply; yet Woolmer, to deflect criticism from the sterility of his bowlers, said he was surprised England did not go for the win.

A couple of winters ago he showed me round the Pakistan Academy in Lahore where he lived much of the year, when not on tour or with his wife Gill in Cape Town. He had all the creature comforts in his apartment inside the complex, including a chef to indulge him, but it was a place short of light and company except for the chowkidars – the gate-keepers. He had always been an outsider, which made it easier for him to break away from the pack to join World Series Cricket or the first England rebel tour of South Africa. He was born in Kanpur, where his father was working, and raised a little in Calcutta. He never put down roots after being sent to boarding school in Kent. Yet you could not call him a mercenary, because he wandered the earth talking about cricket to everyone who would listen, of whatever race. He had learnt only a few words of Hindi when young, but they came in useful when Pakistan's captain Inzamam-ul-Haq strolled in, and the pair embraced and smiled and exchanged greetings with such effusion that it was hard to know how much sincerity was involved.

The last time we talked was ten days before he died, at the Pakistan team's hotel in Port of Spain. He had moved on mentally as their coach. Three years of politicking had got him down. 'When I started I could influence everything,' Woolmer said. 'Now I can influence nothing.' He was not sad, or depressed, however, let alone suicidal. He was not even resigned to becoming a television commentator, a lifestyle which I thought would have suited him. 'I want to coach,' he said, as near emphatically as his softness of tone would allow. He knowingly worked in dangerous waters, with South Africa in the Hansie Cronje years of corruption, then with the team representing a country that is rotten to the political core. Bob Woolmer, though, was imbued with innocent enthusiasm.

Robert Andrew Woolmer: b Kanpur, India, 14 May 1948; d 18 March 2007

I MAY 2007
TOM CARTWRIGHT
A Master of His Craft
David Green

Tom Cartwright was a great medium-pace bowler who, because he played in an era in which sheer pace was increasingly deemed all-important, was picked for only five Tests, a figure which mocks his immense skills. He was also the man responsible for honing the fast-bowling talents of a young Ian Botham, who said about Tom that 'he always had time, always had faith in me. I couldn't have had a better man to teach me'. Tom also played an unwitting part in one of the greatest scandals to rock the game. In 1968–69 he was not fit enough to accept a place on the England tour to South Africa and was replaced by Basil D'Oliveira. The tour was cancelled and South Africa were isolated from the international game.

Tom was initially a batsman who bowled a bit. He made his Warwickshire debut when still almost a boy in 1952, but two years of National Service, allied to an already strong Warwickshire batting order, limited his opportunities. In fact, it was not until 1956 that he played with any regularity. In 1959 he made nearly thirteen hundred runs and took eighty wickets. It was during that summer that I first played against him, when he bowled big inswingers with the high action that characterised his bowling. From half a mile away you would have known it was Tom bowling. However, his acute cricket brain worked out the limitations of a method based purely on inswing – the difficulty of getting leg before decisions and the fact that the ball leaving the bat is more difficult to play than the one coming in. Accordingly, though still using inswing at times, he deliberately limited the amount of it he obtained to a bat's width. He developed an outswinger which, combined with movement either way off the pitch when it helped and complete control of length and line, made him a formidable performer.

Tom broke into the England side in 1964, playing twice against Australia, his debut being at Old Trafford when the Australians made 656 for eight declared. Tom's figures of 77-32-118-2 reflect his accuracy, stamina and guts. Tom's finest moment in Tests was at Trent Bridge in 1965 against South Africa when he would have skittled their powerful batting in the first innings but for Graeme Pollock making a dazzling century. As it was Tom still finished with six for 94. He moved to Somerset in 1970, taking 408 first-class wickets at 18.87 in seven seasons. As Glamorgan coach he was called out of retirement in 1977, responding with one for 46 in the championship against Middlesex.

Tom was a master of his craft. His incredible accuracy caused some people to classify him as 'negative'. On a flat pitch, Tom had two slips and a gully and at least one close fielder on the leg side, with a second short leg posted if there was anything in the pitch. I cannot see how you could be negative if you have five close catchers and bowl every ball at the stumps. For almost all bowlers the outswinger needs to be bowled from close to the stumps and the inswinger from wide on the crease. This gives batsmen a clue to the bowler's intention. Tom, however, could bowl an inswinger from close in and an away swinger from wide, a nasty trick which he passed on to the young Botham.

I have never driven past a pub called The Nag's Head without thinking that Tom's face should be on the sign rather than a horse's.

He gave away absolutely nothing. For my part, I was more concerned with trying to keep Tom out than attempting to hit him anywhere. In March this year Tom suffered a heart attack while out shopping in Neath. Nine days after the attack he was due to have launched his biography, *The Flame Still Burns*. It is a fitting title. Tom was a fine cricketer and his legacy speaks for itself.

Thomas William Cartwright: b Alderman's Green, Coventry, 22 July 1935; d 30 April 2007

28 OCTOBER 2009
DAVID SHEPHERD
From Toby-Jug Batsman to
Much-Respected Umpire
Derek Pringle

Test umpires tend to have ambivalent relationships with players, but with David Shepherd there was no ambiguity. He was quite simply loved and respected by all who met him, which is why the cricket world is suddenly a poorer place following his death. Not many in professional sport are held in such universal regard. Sir Bobby Robson is one, Shep, to give him the moniker most in cricket knew him by, another. Both men had kindly looks, which undoubtedly helped; Robson's crinkly face that of the forgiving parent, Shep's ruddy-cheeked jollity that of a sun-kissed farm worker from another age. But if looks are sometimes deceptive, there was no mistaking the humanity that oozed from their every pore.

Due to the power of television Shep was probably most widely known for his umpiring, his career lasting from 1981 until 2005. Yet he was a handy middle-order batsman for Gloucestershire before that, his lusty thumps, bottom hand to the fore, both a celebration and an indication of his rural Devon roots. I played against him once, in 1979 at Fenner's, for Cambridge against the mighty 'Glos', as you could call them back then. As he strolled to the crease, all pot belly and mutton-chop sideburns, he looked like the picture on a toby jug. But while the entrance was comic, his shots packed power and any sideways sniggers on our part soon turned to bruise-handed admiration. He played in an age when boundary hitting was popular simply because running between the wickets wasn't. According to team-mates, his aversion to physical jerks was legendary and when Les Bardsley, Bristol City's physio-cum-trainer, sent the players on a run, Shep completed most of it on a milk float.

His first-class average of 24.4 is no great shakes these days (though half his career would have been played on uncovered pitches), which is why umpiring, at which he excelled, will be seen as his calling. Like his colleague, Dickie Bird, he had a natural rapport with players, which coupled with fine decision-making, made him the ideal adjudicator, something borne out by his standing in three successive World Cup finals between 1996 and 2003. Great umpiring decisions are rarely recalled even by their beneficiaries, but one thing Shep will be fondly remembered for was his quirk of hopping from foot to foot whenever the scoreboard registered the dreaded 'Nelson'. Most cricketers are superstitious and a score reading 111 (said to represent one of Nelson's eyes, one of his arms, and one of his legs) is thought to bring bad luck. To counteract that, players on the batting side are meant to lift one leg off the ground until the score moves on. Shep never lost the fear and, commendably neutral, would shake a leg for both sides. Inevitably, it became his trademark though unfortunately it gave rise to wannabees such as Billy Bowden, who failed to discern the difference between idiosyncrasy and idiocy.

Shepherd's popularity did not make him immune from criticism. Standing in a Test at Old Trafford in 2001, he missed several no-balls, three of which resulted in wickets as England, losing eight of them in the final session, lost to Pakistan. There was a big hoo-ha and after watching the replays he considered resigning. But most players, including those on the losing side, were phlegmatic: far rather an umpire got decisions right at the business end of the pitch, the batsman's end, than catch a bowler transgressing on the front crease by half an inch. In any case, the unusual alignment of the Old Trafford pitch at the time meant he was looking into the sun as the bowler bowled. The International Cricket Council obviously felt the same, for Shep was the first name on their elite panel when it was announced the following year. Yet undoubted though his excellence as an umpire was, David Shepherd will be remembered most for simply being a genuinely good bloke. As David Graveney, a former team-mate, said yesterday: 'He had a word for everyone, and it was always an encouraging one.' Few memorials come better than that.

**David Robert Shepherd: b Bideford, Devon,
27 December 1940; d 27 October 2009**

6 NOVEMBER 1999
MALCOLM MARSHALL
A Magical Fast Bowler for All Seasons
Mark Nicholas

Moments before midnight on Thursday, Robin Smith telephoned with the numbing news we had feared for most of the week. Malcolm Marshall had died. Cancer of the colon got him during the early summer and, in a remorseless pursuit, nailed him before the autumn leaves finished their fall. He was forty-one years old.

Marshall's last Test match in England was at the Oval in 1991. Smith recalled how he ground out for nearly five hours against typically accurate fast bowling that allowed him no quarter. He remembered vividly how stuck he became with his score at 98 and how Marshall, sensing the unease, altered his field to place another slip and leave just two men on the leg side. Three balls later he bowled a soft half-volley at leg stump which Smith pushed comfortably into the vast open space at mid-wicket. Smith is certain Marshall gave him that hundred. Marshall, to the end, would not have a bit of it.

A remarkable cricketer and a very special person has gone. If there was an element of ruthlessness about Marshall's bowling, there was not a hint of anything but warmth and generosity in his personality. He was a sportsman driven by self-belief, ambition and hope, but always he remained a players' man – forever lifting spirits, experimenting and educating both friend and foe in the nets, suggesting this and demanding that. His high standards set the tone for teams in which he played and coached. It was not always possible for lesser talents to climb the mountain that 'Macko' managed, but it was fun trying and more fun still to watch at first hand his own astonishing deeds.

He was a cricketer of indomitable spirit, immense will, utter dedication and supreme skill. He took 376 Test match wickets and 1,651 in all first-class cricket – 823 of those for Hampshire in a county career which began at the snow-covered racecourse ground in Derby in 1979 and finished when the knackering diet of a four-day county championship and three one-day competitions became too much for him in 1993. Briefly, he then played for Natal in South Africa, leading them to the Castle Cup at the first attempt.

In Barbados, trophy after trophy, honour after honour, came his way. His closest friends, Desmond Haynes and Joel Garner, who were with him through the glory years, were with him in his final moments, as, of course, was Connie, his wife. She said he went peacefully, without pain. His own father had died in a motorcycle accident before the boy had got out of the cot. It was his grandfather, Oscar Welch, who introduced him to the game and played with him day and night. The young Marshall preferred batting – always did, actually, and he could play a bit, too – but learnt in the playground at school that you didn't get a knock unless you bowled out the bloke who was on strike. So he skipped in fifteen yards, hit a few fellas on the head and castled the rest.

By heaven, he could bowl quickly when he chose – Bobby Parks, our wicketkeeper, was thirty-one paces back one day at Portsmouth – and the skidding, screaming bouncer was the most chilling part of his armoury. Yet his real talent was in understanding his opponents, conditions and pitches and in being able to adapt. He was a natural outswinger of the ball and by the late 1980s, when he had mastered the inswinger, he at times appeared almost unplayable.

In 1992 Hampshire were bowled out cheaply by Essex in a crucial Benson and Hedges match. Marshall, who was desperate for a day at Lord's with his beloved adopted county, won the match in minutes by trapping Graham Gooch, John Stephenson and Mark Waugh lbw to leave Essex on the ropes at five for three. He finished with four for 20, the man-of-the-match award and, two months later, the cup itself.

Gooch thought him the finest bowler he played against. Viv Richards calls him the greatest of all fast bowlers – 'the man with the biggest heart and the smartest brain'. For my part, I shall remember the laughter, the dancing eyes, and the incessant, always enthusiastic, chatter. If much of Malcolm characterised the calypso cricketer, much too epitomised the model professional. From Sydney to Southampton, in Barbados, Bournemouth and Bangalore, Malcolm Marshall was a man for all seasons.

Malcolm Denzil Marshall: b Bridgetown, Barbados, 18 April 1958; d 4 November 1999

7 DECEMBER 1999
SYLVESTER CLARKE
Nasty, Brutish and Short
Simon Hughes

The millennium debates rage on to identify the most important man of the century, the most erotic woman and the outstanding competitor. There is little dispute about one sporting issue, though. The West Indian cricketer Sylvester Clarke was the fastest, nastiest bowler who ever lived. Anyone who played – or watched – county cricket in the last twenty-five years will vouch for that.

Surrey, seeking more firepower, signed Clarke speculatively in 1979. In his first match, he reduced Lancashire to three for two before the rains came. In his second, he took four wickets and put two batsmen in hospital. In his third, he demolished Northamptonshire. This was just an aperitif. Clarke went on to terrorise two generations of batsmen, clanging almost as many helmets as he uprooted stumps. He took 942 wickets in all, at an average of 19.52.

An immense man who lifted weights I couldn't even roll, he ambled in off a shortish run and, from a smooth, whirling action generated exceptional pace and a vicious inswinger. This made his yorker as hard to dig out as his bouncer was to avoid. It veered back and followed batsmen too timid to get in line. And there were plenty of those. Indeed, his psychological impact was as great as his physical one. On arrival at the Oval, teams sought a health report on Surrey's opening bowler, hoping to detect some sign of a limp or a late night. Neither was a reliable guide. Clarke invariably stumbled into bed in the early hours and hobbled to the ground forty minutes before the start. But his first over at 11 a.m. was 90 mph chin music.

The first time I faced him, batting at number nine for Middlesex, I made to leave the dressing room without a helmet, thinking the pitch wasn't all that quick. Someone obligingly plonked one on my head. Clarke looked extremely menacing at the end of his run, and, hemmed in by heckling close fielders, I felt something akin to fear. Less of the physical variety, more the potential mortification of being made to look totally incapable, flailing arms and legs around like a demented punk. 'Step back and across, back and across,' I repeated to myself, 'and watch for the bouncer.' I played the first two OK. They hit the bat anyway. 'Let's polish 'em off, Silvers,' one fielder beckoned, and another added: 'Oi, Syl, did you hear what he called you? – *A fat, black git.*'

I knew it was coming this time. I stepped back and across and saw the ball pitch short. Then I lost it. I was vaguely conscious of my flailing arms and legs – just like that demented punk – before the ball crashed into my protected temple, making a horrible reverberating sound. It left a menacing red mark on the Perspex side-piece, a gory reminder of the time I'd been two millimetres of man-made fibre from death. Clarke's reaction to being warned for intimidation was a curt, 'What d'you think this is, a ladies' game?' – followed by another bouncer. This wasn't so much malicious, just that he saw this as the quickest way to get back inside and put his feet up.

He produced frequent devastating spells for Surrey, Barbados and Transvaal, the most influential in the 1984–85 Currie Cup final. His opponents, Northern Transvaal, had prepared a dodgy, green pitch and were rather delighted when they dismissed the might of Transvaal, Graeme Pollock and all, for 232. Clarke responded by taking five for eight and demolishing the hosts for 61. Transvaal won the match by an innings.

He continued to make batsmen jump into the mid-1990s, notably England's in the Bridgetown nets, Clarke wearing trainers with no socks after a night on the tiles. Yet he played only eleven Tests. His dissolute lifestyle and tendency towards injury didn't particularly endear him to the West Indies selectors, who already had Andy Roberts, Michael Holding, Malcolm Marshall and Joel Garner up their sleeves. Of all fast bowlers, Marshall might have been the most gifted, Richard Hadlee the most clinical, and Curtly Ambrose the most economical. But Sylvester Clarke was certainly the most frightening.

Sylvester Theophilus Clarke: b Christ Church, Barbados, 11 December 1954; d 4 December 1999

5 OCTOBER 2011

GRAHAM DILLEY
The Sultan of Swing

Derek Pringle

With his imposing physique and blond good looks, Graham Dilley had the demeanour of a Greek god. Occasionally, when the rhythm was good and his confidence buoyed, he performed like one too, his fast outswingers too good even for batsmen as imposing as Vivian Richards. I played only a handful of Tests with Dill, or Picca, as he was also known; the most memorable of them, at least before reality set in, being against a West Indies side captained by Richards at Lord's in 1988. On an overcast opening day, Dilley, a more controlled bowler than the twenty-year-old upstart who had been called up for an Ashes tour before he had even won his county cap at Kent, had the ball swinging away at pace. None of the batsmen could cope as his opening salvo claimed Gordon Greenidge, Desmond Haynes, Richie Richardson and then the mighty Richards himself as the West Indies slumped to 54 for five. A rout looked likely until your correspondent spilled Gus Logie off him at first slip. Logie took full advantage to make 81 and take West Indies up to 209, a more than competitive total as it happened with a bowling attack comprising Malcolm Marshall, Curtly Ambrose, Courtney Walsh and Patrick Patterson. England lost, but it might have been very different had I not floored that catch off Dill.

Not that he held it against me. A personable man, with a fondness for a pint and a fag, he was, in truth, probably too gentle to be the consummate fast bowler. From the side, though, he had all the attributes to be one, save that which separates the hugely talented from the very best: a rigorous self-belief. Sports psychiatrists were not as prevalent as they are today, but had one managed to purge him of his self-doubt, he would have comfortably doubled his tally of 138 Test wickets and halved the number of niggles that kept him from the field. Even so, he became the undisputed spearhead of England's attack in the mid-1980s. Many talk of his role in the 1981 Ashes miracle at Headingley, where his half-century has almost been forgotten among Ian Botham's pyrotechnics, but his bowling in the 1986–87 series, in which he took sixteen wickets in four Tests, was crucial in preventing Australia bouncing back after England took an early lead.

I first encountered him when we were teenagers picked for the National Association of Young Cricketers South team to play in a cricket festival at Charterhouse School in 1977. Dilley was quick, even then, and I remember fielding at short leg to him as he peppered Ireland's opening batsman about the chest. 'He hates the Irish you know,' I said in a callow attempt to sledge the beleaguered batsman. 'Tell him I'm British then,' came the witty but futile response, as yet another bouncer thundered into his ribs. His bowling action, like his coaching style later on, was a mixture of new and old. The chest-on delivery is all the rage now, but his long delivery stride, with its dragged back foot was from the era of Fred Trueman. It helped Worcestershire win two county championship titles in the late 1980s, though by then the unreliability of his fitness had cost him his England place.

His move into coaching was a welcome one as he had endured hardship after his move from Kent to Worcestershire had cost him the safety net of a benefit year. His penchant for taking his bowlers to the bar for a beer and a chat, when he briefly became England's assistant coach under Duncan Fletcher, was a tried and trusted way of imparting knowledge that went all the way back to Larwood and Voce. Trouble was some of his charges were as thirsty as him, and not for knowledge, which is fine when you are winning but a sacking offence when you are not. He settled for coaching Loughborough University, a job away from the limelight, but then he always did prefer to be away from the glare. His death came as a shock to me as I was not even aware he had been ill, something it seems he had kept from most people. If only he had rated himself as much as others rated him, as a cricketer and a man, he might still be with us.

**Graham Roy Dilley: b Dartford, Kent,
18 May 1959; d 5 October 2011**

19 JANUARY 1998

DAVID BAIRSTOW
Built Like a Muckstack
but Not So Indestructible

Michael Parkinson

We haven't had many wicketkeepers in Yorkshire, only seven or eight in a hundred years or more. David Bairstow was one of them. He understood he was part of a great tradition but wasn't overawed by it. In fact, not much fazed David Bairstow. Or so we thought.

I remember when he came as a schoolboy into the Yorkshire team, which in those days was not so much a cricket team, more an academy of cricketing knowledge run by Brian Close and Raymond Illingworth where it was accepted sprogs kept their opinions to themselves until they had earned the right to address such illustrious company. I was in the dressing room when Brian Close returned in foul humour having been given out lbw. As the captain addressed his players on the subject of blind umpires they pretended to busy themselves with other tasks to avoid catching his eye and being drawn inevitably into the tirade. All save the young Bairstow, who gazed in wonder at his captain in full spate. As he paused for breath Close looked at Bairstow and said: 'And what does tha' think, young 'un?' Bairstow said: 'I think tha' goes on a bit.' He didn't muck about with the niceties either as a player or a man. If the ball was up he smacked it; if he didn't like you he told you so.

A true son of the soil that shaped him. Built like a muckstack and indestructible. So we thought.

When he finished playing county cricket he came down to Maidenhead and Bray now and again and helped us out. It was enlightening to see him with our players: encouraging, cajoling and sometimes bollocking them to better things. He played every game like a Test match. It was the only way he knew. He was the best of company, intelligent and perceptive in everything he did and said except when it came to business ventures and dealing with Yorkshire County Cricket Club. He felt snubbed by Yorkshire and no amount of persuasion and arguing by his friends could convince him otherwise. It was sad to see such a dedicated Yorkshireman at odds with the institution he loved and admired beyond all else apart from the family.

In the past couple of years I detected a sadness in him, an uncertainty about what the future might hold. The eternal predicament of athletes is not that they retire too soon but that they retire at all. Yet David had been working as a commentator for the BBC and was doing well. It wasn't a fortune but it kept him in touch with the game he loved. I saw him during the last cricket season. He had put on weight but seemed as vigorous and robust as ever. When I was told he had committed suicide, I said: 'Don't be daft. Not Bluey.' Not that strong, fearless, laughing mate I knew. Now all I can think is, 'Why, old lad, why?'

David Leslie Bairstow: b Bradford, West Yorkshire, 1 September 1951; d 5 January 1998

13 NOVEMBER 2011
PETER ROEBUCK
A Man Destined Not
to Live an Easy Life
Derek Pringle

Peter Roebuck possessed one of the keenest, most analytical minds of his generation, and one not easily swayed once made up. What made him consider all outcomes bleak enough to launch himself from the sixth floor of a Cape Town hotel on Saturday night is not yet fully understood, only that the fall ended a life as troubled as it was rich with talent. Suicide is something Roebuck predicted would never take him, though those who had known him since his youth were less certain. In his foreword for the reprint of David Frith's book on cricket suicides, *Silence of the Heart*, he wrote: 'Some people have predicted a gloomy end for this writer. One former colleague said so to my face in September 1986. It will not be so. The art is to find other things that matter just as much as cricket, which stretch you just as far. Certainly a man needs beliefs. Principles are not enough. But belief can spring from satisfaction in his own work, for to believe in your self is an act of faith. Since 1983 I have led a stable, remarkably untroubled life, and such vicissitudes as have occurred have been connected with cricket form rather than temperament.'

Roebuck wrote that early in 2001, a few months before the scandal of him caning three 19-year-old boys in his care in Taunton came to court and he was forced to admit common assault. Like his controversial move in 1986, when he replaced Somerset's overseas players Vivian Richards and Joel Garner with Martin Crowe, a tempestuous time that saw him branded as 'Judas' by Ian Botham, who left Somerset in protest, the stain never really faded. Time usually dilutes such things but with Roebuck, who shunned England as a result to become an Australian citizen based in Bondi, you sensed these were seminal moments in which the shame and controversy were accreting with age not dissipating.

Suggestions that he was gay have circulated since his playing days, but if true he has never acknowledged it to anyone I know. In any case, he did not crave partners on an equal footing but followers. An intense, driven man, Roebuck was never destined to have an easy life and in a way he resented those who did. He despised sloppiness of any kind, though that contradicts his hero worship of R.J.O. Meyer, the controversial founder of Millfield School in Somerset, where Roebuck attended on a scholarship. Meyer, a former Somerset cricketer, would think nothing of gambling school fees on the stock market or a horse race, any winnings providing extra bursaries for the talented but less well heeled. Roebuck acquired Meyer's educationalist zeal, setting up scholarships for the underprivileged in South Africa, but not his raffish touch.

Roebuck was a fine cricketer; a brave, organised batsman who could have considered himself unlucky not to have been one of Graham Gooch's opening partners for England in the late 1980s. He probably came closest when asked to captain an England side, in which your correspondent also played, in two one-day matches against Holland in Amsterdam during 1989. England lost the first game but won the second, though the lack of faith in Roebuck was immediately apparent when Mickey Stewart, the coach, rushed up to journalists after the defeat and told them to discount everything Roebuck had said at the press conference.

He had the sharpest of minds (he took a double first in law at Cambridge) and, when the mood overcame him, a lacerating tongue as well. A brilliant writer on cricket for among others the *Sunday Times* and the *Sydney Morning Herald*, he was once accosted by Mark Nicholas, who penned a regular column himself at the time and who informed Roebuck that they were the best cricket writers around. 'Who told you that,' quipped Roebuck, 'your mother?'

I first encountered him on an Oxbridge tour of Australia in 1979–80, where he and Paul Parker, both playing club cricket in Sydney, were drafted in to strengthen our team. Roebuck's disdain for most of the opposition (he was a Somerset regular at this stage who had shared record batting stands with Viv Richards) was obvious and in one game against Monash University, he had completed at least two crosswords at second slip before we had bowled them out. An acquaintance who played cricket at Cambridge with both of us once said Roebuck was destined to be a discontented soul, as a single lifetime was not long enough for him to achieve his ambitions. That he has not seen even one through suggests that any hopes he still had were suddenly replaced by an insurmountable wall of fear.

Peter Michael Roebuck: b Oddington, Oxfordshire, 6 March 1956; d 12 November 2011

3 JUNE 2002
HANSIE CRONJE
Golden Boy with a
Heart of Darkness

Hansie Cronje was South Africa's most successful cricket captain and regarded as a national hero until he became implicated in a bribery, corruption and match-fixing scandal that not only wrecked his career but brought shame to the game internationally. Such was his stature in the world of cricket, as a player, a captain and a sporting ambassador for the newly democratic South Africa, that the initial allegations by Indian police in 2000 – that he had accepted bribes from bookmakers for fixing international matches – were greeted with disbelief and derision. Cronje, a born-again Christian, at first denied the charges; but two days later he confessed, first to his pastor and then to the South African cricket authorities, that he had 'not been entirely honest'. The ensuing furore led to a commission of inquiry chaired by Edwin King, a retired judge.

It was an ignominious end to the career of a cricketer regarded as an inspirational captain of his country. The ten days of hearings by the King commission in Cape Town led to revelations of the murkier side of professional cricket, in which large sums of money provided by a sinister web of bookmakers changed hands to fix the results of matches. In his evidence to the widely televised commission, Cronje demonstrated the enigmatic side of his character, claiming at one stage that he had 'allowed Satan and the world to dictate terms to me'. Other evidence, however, suggested that the South African captain had made the running in his contacts with bookmakers. He finally admitted that he had received some £100,000 in dirty money and had offered bribes of £15,000 each to two members of his team to underperform in a one-day match against India. The fact that both men, Herschelle Gibbs and Henry Williams, were non-white players – Cape Coloureds, in old South African parlance – was probably the most damning in the eyes of many. Cronje had pledged his full support to South African cricket's development programme designed to bring to the first-class game young black talent.

King made it clear that he did not believe Cronje was telling the whole truth to the commission, a suspicion confirmed when it later emerged that he had overseas bank accounts containing substantial funds which could not have been derived from his salary and match fees. He also admitted that he had received £5,000 and a leather jacket from a South African bookmaker to contrive a result in a seemingly dead Test between South Africa and England in January 2000. Cronje was banned for life by the South African Cricket Board, a move later endorsed by the International Cricket Council. Such was the damage he was deemed to have inflicted that he was prohibited from any involvement in the game, even coaching or becoming a commentator – though these last two restrictions were later lifted. The once revered name of a national hero became a byword for cheating and chicanery.

In 1993, he had been appointed vice-captain to Kepler Wessels for the tour in Australia. He took over when the captain was injured and had to leave the field. South Africa won the thrilling second Test in Sydney by five runs, securing for Cronje and his team a devoted following which was not to diminish until his downfall.

He succeeded Wessels as captain in 1994–95 when New Zealand toured South Africa, proving his stature as an inspirational leader with a bold declaration which led to a series-winning game. England were vanquished in 1995–96 – the first series they had lost to South Africa since 1930–31 – and Pakistan and Zimbabwe were overwhelmed.

Rarely showing emotion on the field, though he was possessed of a sharp sense of humour and fun off it, Cronje could not disguise his anguish when South Africa were knocked out of the 1999 World Cup in the semi-final against Australia at Edgbaston with a final-ball run-out. The match was described by commentators and players as one of the most thrilling in the history of the sport; but for Cronje, it was the end of a dream he had nurtured since his childhood – to lead South Africa to a World Cup victory. Perhaps it was no coincidence that, from that time on, disturbing questions about Cronje's ethics began to circulate in the cricketing world. The Indian police, basing their case on tapped telephone calls, alleged that Cronje had been involved with bookmakers in match-fixing shortly after the South African team returned from their Indian tour in April 2000.

Cronje captained the national side in fifty-three Tests – more than any other South African captain – twenty-seven of which were won, fifteen drawn and eleven lost. As a batsman, though vulnerable against pace, he was one of the finest players of spin bowling in the world, surpassed only, perhaps, by Sachin Tendulkar.

Wessel Johannes Cronje: b Bloemfontein, Orange Free State Province,
25 September 1969; d 1 June 2002

23 JANUARY 2000
E.W. SWANTON
Sort of a Cricket Person
Scyld Berry

E.W. Swanton was the doyen of English cricket writers and of cricket writers in English. He attended the Lord's Test of 1930 and declared to the end that it was the best cricket match he had seen, graced as it was by hundreds from Percy Chapman and Duleepsinhji and a double hundred by Don Bradman. And all but seventy seasons later he was still attending Lord's, and writing columns for the *Daily Telegraph*, which remained the embodiment of cricket common sense.

He was High Church and, occasionally, high-handed. When he was at the peak of his powers, he would deliver a close-of-play summary on *Test Match Special* which was as lucid and authoritative as his prose. Before delivering it, he needed to lubricate his throat with a whisky on the rocks, and woe betide the cricket ground which did not have any ice. His summary – sometimes after he had done ball-by-ball broadcasting during the day, but his sole contribution by the end of his radio career – was usually prefaced by a solemn 'it has been an absorbing day's play and I shall start by reading the card'. Denis Compton was always 'Cumpton' and Geoff Boycott was 'Boycutt' – and sometimes names a good deal worse.

Swanton, who played a handful of first-class matches for Middlesex as a batsman in the 1930s, got his first major cricket job on the *Evening Standard*. He nearly went to Australia in 1932–33, and claimed that Bodyline – the bowling of fast short-pitched balls at the batsman's head some forty years ahead of its time – would never have happened if he had been there, instead of lesser mortals who could not report the game to readers in England with his lucidity and authority.

During the Second World War, he was taken prisoner in Singapore and was said to have behaved with bravery and dignity in a Japanese PoW camp from 1942 to 1945 while some around him did not. He had a battered copy of a 1939 *Wisden* to cling to during his imprisonment, if cricket was not a large enough part of his life already.

After the War, he became the *Daily Telegraph's* cricket correspondent – and in some style. There was more than his whisky and ice to consider for the young men (and, more rarely, young women) who were employed to be his amanuensis. When he travelled to the West Indies, for instance, he alone of the cricket correspondents had to have a bunk bed on the flight to North America. Pakistan and India were not countries he toured: when England went there, the late Michael Melford of the *Sunday Telegraph* had to cover for him.

On arriving in the West Indies for M.C.C.'s (or England's) 1953–54 tour, he began his first story with the words: 'L.E.G. Ames (manager), L. Hutton (captain)' with a list of all the players to follow. Then: 'The above have arrived in Barbados.' J.J. Warr, sometime correspondent for the *Sunday Telegraph*, likened Swanton's style to 'a combination of the Ten Commandments and Enid Blyton'. As with many comments about 'The Doyen', it needed to be taken with a pinch of humorous affection.

The West Indies and their cricketers – Garry Sobers and the three Ws of Frank Worrell, Everton Weekes and Clyde Walcott, in particular – were his especial love. For a time, he had a second home in Barbados before selling it and holidaying at Sandy Lane, where he indulged in another of his affections, golf. His closeness to the West Indies helped him to take a more progressive line on South Africa at the time of the Basil D'Oliveira affair than many of his colleagues. He raised and managed a couple of his own touring teams to the West Indies in 1956 and 1961, including some famous cricketers like Frank Tyson. His first cricket books were mainly records of England tours to Australia and the West Indies. As he grew to be older and ever more The Doyen, the titles of his books reflected his importance: *Swanton in Australia* for instance, and *As I Said At The Time*, or *The Essential E.W. Swanton*.

He would advise his amanuenses and any other prospective young cricket-writers to aim for clarity above all else and advocated the reading of Winston Churchill's prose to this end. While his memory may have lapsed a little with age, his columns in the *Daily Telegraph* never fell from their high standard, even though he continued to write for twenty-five years after his retirement in 1975.

It would have been fitting if he had been elected president of M.C.C. after his decades of service on various committees, most latterly the arts and library, but while his great friend Sir George ('Gubby') Allen was elected, 'Jim' never was. His avuncular style and unrivalled knowledge would have been well suited to the post, and he was after all cricket's establishment personified.

One of his many amanuenses was John Woodcock, who accompanied him by ship to Australia in 1950–51 before becoming cricket correspondent of *The Times*: he now succeeds to the title of 'doyen'. Another was Daphne Surfleet, who became Mrs Richie Benaud. I, too, filled the job, if only for eight days in 1973, though not for any want of patrician kindness on his part.

He married Ann in 1958 and lived for the latter half of his life in Sandwich, Kent, but died without issue. Probably nobody has written more published words on one subject than he did over seventy years, and certainly not with such clarity and perception. For cricketers and readers about the game of games, this century is already poorer than the last.

**Ernest William Swanton: b Forest Hill, London,
11 February, 1911; d 22 January, 2000**

2 JANUARY 2013
CHRISTOPHER MARTIN-JENKINS
The Voice of an English Summer
Derek Pringle

Had Christopher Martin-Jenkins been fictional he would have been one of the great comic inventions, a hybrid of Basil Fawlty and Bertie Wooster. Instead, CMJ, for whom humour – intended or otherwise – was never far away, became one of cricket's most famous and enduring voices through four decades spent covering the game for journalism's holy trinity: the BBC, the *Daily Telegraph* and *The Times*.

The accolades were universally affectionate towards the man many considered the voice of the English summer during his long service with *Test Match Special*. Jonathan Agnew, the BBC's cricket correspondent and a near-constant companion of CMJ's in the commentary box for the past two decades, said: 'CMJ was one of cricket's most respected writers and broadcasters. With media now preferring the views of former Test match cricketers, Christopher's authority and respect was not gained from a high-profile playing career, but a deep-rooted love of the game linked to a strong protective instinct which helped him earn the most coveted position of president of M.C.C. Considering the years he worked as editor of *The Cricketer* magazine, and as correspondent for the BBC twice, the *Daily Telegraph* and *The Times*, and forty years commentating on *Test Match Special* and the many books he wrote, it is doubtful that anyone has contributed more in a lifetime to the overall coverage of cricket.'

He continued to contribute columns to *The Times* until as recently as Monday, when he wrote about the death of Tony Greig: 'It was probably for him a merciful release because the late stage of any cancer is often hell on earth.'

Cricket fans will remember him for his prose and radio work but my abiding memories, apart from his generosity in allowing me the chance to write for *The Cricketer* and then the *Daily Telegraph*, where Mark Nicholas and I alternated a column in the late 1980s, are all humorous ones, with CMJ usually the butt of the joke. His off-air life was chaotic, fuelled by his insistence in filling every waking moment with some task or other, which meant he was habitually late for everything. He was forever rushing and forgetting things, often with calamitous results. Once, while running late for a charity golf day in Barbados, he failed to secure his golf bag on the back seat of the Mini Moke he was using as transport. As he rushed to make his tee time, CMJ deposited clubs at various roundabouts en route. He noticed that half the bag was missing only once he had reached his destination, whereupon he zoomed off to retrace his steps in an unsuccessful attempt to recover the equipment.

On another occasion, covering a Test match in London, he eschewed the usual hotels and stayed at the Oxford and Cambridge Club. Whether the new venue disorientated him, or the potency of the club brandy brought on short-term memory loss, he was late on parade the next day having gone to Lord's for a match taking place at the Oval.

Having been educated at Marlborough and Fitzwilliam College, Cambridge, he was that rare thing in modern British life, an old-fashioned gentleman. If he did lose his temper, which was not often, he did so with gadgets rather than people. This country no longer turns out many like CMJ. He will be sadly missed.

Christopher Dennis Alexander Martin-Jenkins: b Peterborough, 20 January, 1945; d 1 January, 2013

1 NOVEMBER 1993
GEORGE POPE
The Artful Keeper of Life's Mysteries
Michael Parkinson

The death of George Henry Pope caused barely a ripple in the national press. Where it was noted it stated that Pope, the Derbyshire all-rounder whose career was interrupted by the War, died peacefully at his home aged eighty-two. Those who knew him and played against him will mourn a much more considerable man than can be dismissed in a few lines. He was a magnificent all-round cricketer and there can be little doubt that had it not been for the War years he would have played for England many times. In 1938, *Wisden* said of him: 'Good judges forecast a brilliant future for this tall, hard-working cricketer who personifies the true spirit of the game.' On his return to county cricket in 1947 he joined forces with Cliff Gladwin, Bill Copson and a youngster called Les Jackson to form one of the best seam attacks ever possessed by a county side. Pope's comeback only lasted a couple of seasons but in his last – 1948 – he became the first player to reach the double, taking one hundred wickets at 17.24 and scoring 1,152 runs at an average of 38.40. He went into the leagues, first Lancashire and then Yorkshire, where he didn't so much play cricket as conduct master classes.

When you look back at your sporting life you remember the key figures in its development. In my case they were my father, Webb Swift, who taught me cricket at school, and George Henry Pope. The difference between my father, Webb Swift and Mr Pope was that the first two were on my side and the other was not. What I learnt from Mr Pope was achieved the hard way, which is to say facing him at Bramall Lane on a grassy wicket and Pope armed with both a new ball and a tame umpire. 'How's Mabel's bad leg?' he would ask the umpire. Flattered by the great man's concern for his sickly wife, astonished he should remember her name and her rheumatic joints, the umpire was bound to give sympathetic consideration to Mr Pope's appeals for lbw. He was also influenced, as was the batsman, by George Henry's non-stop commentary on proceedings. He would rap you on the pads, look ruefully down the wicket and say to himself: 'Nice little leg-cutter that, George. Just did a bit too much, perhaps. What do you think, Mr Umpire?' And the poor besotted creature was bound to agree, as he invariably did the next time Mr Pope struck the pads and this time bellowed a demand for lbw.

When you played against Sheffield you actually took on Mr Pope's XI. He ran things. It would start in the dressing room before the game began when he would visit to greet our professional. A gentlemanly gesture you might think. In fact it was designed to put the fear of God up the opposition. Our professional at that time was Ellis Robinson, late of Yorkshire and Somerset and an old sparring partner of Pope's. 'Fancy thi' chances, Ellis?' Pope would inquire. 'Tha' nivver could bowl,' Ellis would reply: 'Looks a bit green out there. You might be lucky to get fifty,' George would say. 'I just might give thi' some stick today.' On one occasion Pope bowled us out for under fifty, taking eight wickets in the process. Ellis survived unbeaten with a dozen runs. As he took off his pads in the pavilion he uttered the immortal line: 'Nivver could bowl that Popey.'

The point about facing George Pope was that it was the ultimate examination for any young cricketer. There were times when he would tell his team: 'I could bowl out England on this track.' It was not an idle boast. He had a relaxed action and a high relaxed delivery and total command of line and length. He bowled outswing and inswing, snapped the ball back from outside off stump and had a lethal leg-cutter. He learnt the leg-cutter from the great S.F. Barnes. When he retired Barnes settled in Derbyshire and asked if he might sometimes have a net at the county ground. Sam Cadman, the Derbyshire coach, said he could do so if he showed a young promising quick bowler called Pope how to bowl the leg-cutter. So the great man taught Pope what he knew but made him first promise that he would not tell anyone else until he (Pope) had retired from the game. George kept his promise and it wasn't until after his retirement that he told the young Alec Bedser what Barnes had taught him. Thus are life's mysteries handed down.

He loved playing against Yorkshire and delighted in telling the story about batting against Hedley Verity with the redoubtable Brian Sellars standing intimidatingly close at silly mid-on. Pope, who was a formidable striker of a cricket ball, decided to remove the threat. He went down the wicket to Verity and hit him ferociously through mid-wicket, just missing Sellars. The Yorkshire captain became angry. 'I think you deliberately tried to hit me then,' he said, accusingly. 'Just stay where you are Mr Sellars and you'll be in no doubt about the next one,' said Pope.

George Pope played once for England, against South Africa in 1947. Many who were less talented played a lot more games for their country, and George Pope knew it. His legacy is that there is a generation of young cricketers – now getting on in years – prepared to testify that he was the best bowler they faced. He was a master of his craft and not many of us will go to our graves with that as our epitaph.

**George Henry Pope: b Tibshelf, Derbyshire,
27 January 1911; d 29 October 1993**